SEARCHING FOR HEROES, SCOUNDRELS, STAR-GAZERS, AND A MERMAID QUEEN

QUESTS

PAUL SPENCER SOCHACZEWSKI

Best-selling author of *EarthLove*
and A *Conservation Notebook*

EXPLORER'S EYE PRESS

GENEVA, SWITZERLAND

Also by
Paul Spencer Sochaczewski

Fiction
Redheads
EarthLove
Exceptional Encounters

Non-Fiction
"Look Here, Sir, What a Curious Bird"
A Conservation Notebook
Searching for Ganesha
Dead, But Still Kicking
An Inordinate Fondness for Beetles
Share Your Journey
Distant Greens
The Sultan and the Mermaid Queen
Malaysia: Heart of Southeast Asia

The Five-Book Non-Fiction Series
Curious Encounters of the Human Kind
Myanmar (Burma)
Indonesia
Himalaya
Borneo
Southeast Asia

———◆———

Co-authored with Jeffrey McNeely
Soul of the Tiger
Eco-Bluff Your Way to Instant Environmental Credibility

Praise for Quests

"Since the Age of Discovery, Western travelers have sought to disenchant the world, to slay its dragons, undermine its gods and ghosts and rationalize away its mysteries. *Quests* does the very opposite, engaging other people on their own terms and restoring to the world the sense of wonder and magic that they retain and we have lost. Paul Spencer Sochaczewski's *Quests* is the absorbing tale of one man's personal odysseys, at once humbling and reveling in the sheer exuberant dottiness of life."

— Nigel Barley, author of *Island of Demons* and *Coronation Chicken*, former curator for Southeast Asia, British Museum

"Full of 'good heart' journalism and surprising insights. There is much to be learned from these finely wrought personal tales of quests in search of … well, just about everything that is mysterious, thought-provoking, exotic, and sometimes just plain bonkers. Paul Spencer Sochaczewski doesn't position this as an autobiography, but this book is a snapshot album of a life well curated, a blueprint for other would-be idea explorers who want to finally (it's never too late) chase the end of the rainbow."

— David Hallmark, fellow, Linnean Society and Royal Geographical Society; co-author of *Alfred Russel Wallace: On the Origins of a Theory*

"Cosmically curious, Paul Spencer Sochaczewski is always a surprising guide into strange encounters and lingering mysteries. If you are interested in stories about the gods, poking into family history, adventuring across the globe or around your living room, you will want to read this book."

— Thomas Bass, author of *The Eudaemonic Pie, The Spy Who Loved Us,* and *Return to Fukushima*

"In the annals of storytelling, from the epics of Homer to the mytho-poetics of modern adventure, one motif stands tall and unwavering — the Hero's Journey. It is a narrative arc that transcends cultures and time, weaving its way through the fabric of human experience. As a quester of both the physical and metaphysical realms, I find myself drawn to this timeless pattern, not just in the grand adventures of first descents of wild rivers, or first ascents of mountains, but in the every-day quests that shape our lives.

"This is why the new book by Paul Spencer Sochaczewski, *Quests*, is so vital, important, and inspirational.

"The Hero's Journey, famously elucidated by Joseph Campbell, is a blueprint for transformation and self-discovery. We are all heroes in our own stories, navigating the unknown, confronting challenges, and striving for growth.

"Consider the 24 personal quests presented in *Quests*, from ghosts to gods, mermaid queens to a purported Lost Tribe of Israel. The hero's journey is not confined to physical feats or epic battles. It is a journey of the soul, a quest for meaning and purpose in a world fraught with challenges and uncertainties. It is about embracing the full spectrum of human experience — the joy and the sorrow, the triumphs and the setbacks — and emerging stronger and wiser on the other side.

"Quests are reminders that within each of us lies the power to tran-scend our limitations and shape our own destiny. Let us not discount the importance of the small, everyday quests that define our lives. Let us embrace the hero's journey in all its forms — from the grand ad-ventures that take us to the farthest reaches of the earth to the quiet moments of introspection that shape our inner landscapes. For in the end, it is not the size or scope of the quest that matters, but the courage and conviction with which we embark upon it."

— Richard Bangs, author of *The Art of Living Dangerously: True Stories from a Life on the Edge*, co-founder of Sobek Expeditions, named by Explorersweb as one of the "100 Great Explorers of the Last 100 Years"

"Paul Spencer Sochaczewski never travels in straight lines. He goes where his imagination and curiosity lead him, which is to places, people, books, and stories that fill him with wonder. He writes with grace and purpose. The winners are his readers, who in a book such as this one can grasp his fine mind and endless energy to reinterpret the known world."

— Matthew Stevenson, contributing editor for *Harper's Magazine*, author of *Biking with Bismarck* and *Donald Trump's Circus Maximus and Joe Biden's Excellent Adventure*

"*Quests* is a new kind of guidebook for the adventure-seeking traveler with a mission.

"People travel for various reasons. Some seek to soak up the sun and sip cocktails by the pool, others to tick off famous sights like Angkor Wat, while others are happy to wander like an aimless leaf in the wind and 'see what happens.'

"But Paul Spencer Sochaczewski is an inspirational example of those curious people who travel with a purpose.

"In his latest book, Sochaczewski calls these goal-oriented adventures 'quests.' He sets out to investigate mysteries that may seem too distant, too complex, too esoteric for many of us. I recommend the clear-eyed voyager reads *Quests* to inspire a richer and more fulfilling personal travel experience."

— Bill Dalton, author of *Indonesia Handbook*, founder of Moon Travel Guides

"Paul Spencer Sochaczewski is a remarkable traveller, exploring exotic places and discovering memorable, unheralded people. In this latest recounting of his fascinating physical and mental journeys, he combines his insights of worldly wisdom with sardonic humor about life's absurdities. A most enjoyable and challenging book, a wonderful voyage with a very special guide."

— Daniel Warner, author of *An Ethic of Responsibility in International Relations*

"Paul Spencer Sochaczewski's latest book, *Quests,* is personal travel writing of the highest quality — a model of journalistic skill.

"During his purposeful quests over wide swathes of tropical Asia he manages to find, and make sense of, a homeless wannabe emperor, a Philippines politician who used love potions to get elected, a man-hating female vampire ghost who wanted to follow him home, the mermaid queen who is the consort of modern Indonesian sultans, the allure of coffee enhanced by civet droppings, the challenges of being the (almost) last shaman of Malaysian Borneo, and the discipline of training monastic jumping cats in Burma.

"As a diplomat and foreign correspondent working in Asia, I long ago realized how a conventional financial and geopolitical analysis of Southeast Asia could carry me only so far. Writers like Sochaczewski (with 20 books about Asia) have made a major contribution to our understanding of the cultural curry of this important and ever-fascinating corner of the world. He has a terrier-like tenacity to pursue legends, contacts, and hidden facts in his often decades-long pursuit of quests that surprise, challenge, and delight us. Sochaczewski is blessed with a mind capable of illuminating rarely imagined insights; he sees the world through a startlingly refreshing and insightful prism. He joins a fraternity of skilled chroniclers and explorers, some from the past, like Joseph Conrad, and other more contemporary writers, including William Dalrymple and Paul Theroux."

— James Clad, author of *Behind the Myth: Business, Money, and Power in Southeast Asia;* co-author of *After the Crusade: American Foreign Policy for the Post-Superpower Age;* former staff correspondent for *Far Eastern Economic Review;* former United States deputy assistant secretary of defense for Asia

"An important ingredient of happiness can be a sense of purpose — of having a goal and setting out to achieve it. Paul Spencer Sochaczewski employs the useful term 'quests' for such enterprises, and in this book, he documents a few of his own — exotic, often fascinating, sometimes bordering on the fantastical. All are recounted in lively fashion. His accounts encourage you, the reader, to break out of your usual patterns and set out on your own quests for illumination and adventure. This could well make a difference to your life."

— Richard Stevens, former chair of Association for Humanistic Psychology, author of *Understanding the Self and Personal Worlds*, lead psychologist for BBC TV's *Making Slough Happy*

Published by:
Explorer's Eye Press
Geneva, Switzerland

Editor and Project Manager: Marla Markman, MarlaMarkman.com
Cover and Interior Design: Kelly Cleary, kellymaureencleary@gmail.com

Publisher's Cataloging-in-Publication data

Names: Sochaczewski, Paul Spencer, author.
Title: Quests : searching for heroes , scoundrels , stargazers , and a mermaid queen / Paul Spencer Sochaczewski.
Description: Includes bibliographical references. | Geneva, Switzerland: Explorer's Eye Press, 2024.
Identifiers: ISBN: 978-2-940573-43-1 (paperback) | 978-2-940573-44-8 (ebook)
Subjects: LCSH Sochaczewski, Paul Spencer--Travel. | Indonesia--Description and travel. | Southeast Asia--Description and travel. | Family. | BISAC BIOGRAPHY & AUTOBIOGRAPHY / Adventurers & Explorers | BIOGRAPHY & AUTOBIOGRAPHY / Memoirs | TRAVEL / Asia / Southeast
Classification: LCC DS620.2 .S63 2024 | DDC 915.9804--dc23

Note: Several of these true encounters were written years or decades ago; some of the statistics might be out of date.

Printed in the United States of America

DEDICATION

When I worked in advertising in Singapore, one of my copywriters came up with this line for a new chocolate bar: "The world is filled with sweeties and nuts."

In that spirit, this book of personal quests is dedicated to the patient people who have encouraged me along the journey and to the exceptional people — some dedicated, some frustrated, some idealistic, some downright gonzo — with whom I've crossed paths and who are profiled in these stories.

And, of course, let's not forget the dreamers. As T.E. Lawrence wrote:

"All men dream, but not equally. Those who dream by night in the dusty recesses of their minds, wake in the day to find that it was vanity; but the dreamers of the day are dangerous men, for they may act on their dreams with open eyes, to make them possible."

Author's Note

The Thais say that when a person reaches his or her sixth cycle, which corresponds to a less-dramatic-sounding 72 years in Western calculations, the lucky individual is perceived to have acquired wisdom and should henceforth be accorded appropriate respect.

It is also said, by less generous commentators, that at such an advanced age a person has ridden his bike over the mountain's summit and is headed downhill, fast.

I don't speculate which of those options is valid. All I can say is that I'm publishing this book several years after my sixth cycle, and I allow myself the luxury to reminisce.

If there is a recurring theme in this book it is that life never stops presenting us with choices. Some call these temporary roadblocks problems, others, challenges. I consider these forks-in-the road opportunities. You go through one door (which shuts firmly behind you), and you enter a changed reality. If it's a fictional story, you might call it the Narnia Wardrobe Effect or Alice's Rabbit Hole. In real life, a chosen path is simply evidence of life moving at its own pace. Surprises smack you in the face, and you must deal with unsuspected idiosyncrasies, unwanted dramas, and edgy encounters. Take more steps, and other doors appear, and you choose one to go through. And on. And on.

But we have some control over which portals we open. To give these gateways a noble-sounding name, we might call them quests. They are the backbone of all great fables — the *Ramayana*, the *Odyssey*, the *Ring* cycle, and the *Wizard of Oz*. According to philosopher Joseph Campbell, such quests — the search for an explanation, an achievement, a place, a meaning, a memory — are the building blocks of the "hero's journey." And while they apply to Luke Skywalker and Don Quixote, they equally apply to you and me.

Quests do not have to involve travels to distant lands. They can be pragmatic and close to home — earning a college degree, starting a business, learning to windsurf, visiting Paris, mastering the art of puff pastry, giving long-term comfort to an ailing relative, or birthing a baby (more on this later).

Whatever path you take, you will try to avoid the frustration of catawampus, in which life ignores your best intentions and events take an unwanted turn. As the saying goes, "if you want to make God laugh, tell her your plans."

But not all quests need be clearly signed to lead to a specific destination or goal. You could engage in coddiwomple, a travel in a purposeful manner toward a vague destination. And sometimes you just need to go with the flow and follow the advice of baseball sage Yogi Berra: "When you come to a fork in the road, take it."

All the stories in this book are true. They do not have gravitas or legacy on a grand scale, but they are my stories, my quests, the results of my own (admittedly often esoteric) curiosity.

What quests have you been up to recently?

Table of Contents

In Search of…
ENIGMAS

Swimming to Waltzing Banana Island

It's Everywhere. It's Nowhere.
It's Dancing in Three-Quarter Time.

Travel & Leisure

It's an island. It's an idea. It's hidden. It may exist only on
top-secret CIA maps or in my imagination.

EN-ROUTE TO PULAU VALSE PISANG, INDONESIA

Some people with stardust in their eyes and too much absinthe
in their veins spend their lives searching for Atlantis or Eldo-
rado. Adventurers windsurf across the Pacific, while true believers
fight for a cause. Other men and women seek an elusive metaphor,
like Peter Matthiessen's snow leopard.

I too have a particular quest. I'm searching for "Waltzing Banana
Island."

"Waltzing Banana Island," or to put it in its correct Indonesian-

French nomenclature, "Pulau Valse Pisang," is a tiny speck of land in far eastern Indonesia. My search for the island is devoid of socially redeeming value; I'm simply intrigued how it got its name. A misspelling of the Dutch *"valsche,"* which would make it the *"False Banana Island"*? A secret, tropical hideaway for Carmen Miranda? An abundance of fruit trees or a crescent-shape? Or, more romantically, maybe it was named by French explorers aboard the *Astrolabe* who charted eastern Indonesian waters in the mid-19th century? Since the banana is a euphemism throughout Indonesia for the male sexual organ, perhaps the lonely French sailors found the local lovelies *très charmantes*, musically inclined, and welcoming.

How did this quest begin?

Several years ago, I was in the library of the Royal Geographical Society in London, glancing at a map of eastern Indonesia, and saw a rather large-font designation for Pulau Valse Pisang. The land mass it related to was just a pinprick. Why such visibility for such a tiny land mass? And why such a peculiar name?

There are certainly worse travel strategies than to visit places with evocative names that purr with history and incense: I've visited places simply because their name beckons, like a geographical siren's song. There's Sumatra, Java, and Borneo; Malacca, Mandalay, and Makassar; Pondicherry, Kathmandu, and Ayutthaya. Not to mention the rivers: Ganges, Yangtze, and Irrawaddy. Mahakam and Mekong.

And now, Pulau Valse Pisang.

But before I could visit it, I had to first find it.

Back to the Royal Geographical Society, where I pored over old maps and atlases. Some of the tattered Dutch charts listed the place with the French-inspired "valse." But confusingly, some of the English maps used the Dutch word "valsche." About 50-50.

The most helpful source was the "Official Standard Names for Indonesia," which was published by the CIA in February 1968. This phone-book-thick tome lists several Valse Pisang islands. The one

I decided was my Dancing Banana Island is at S 2° 08' – E 130° 54'.

It is located at the southern edge of a region known as Raja Ampat, a vast sea off the western coast of the island of New Guinea, dotted with islands and home to the world's richest coral reefs.

I inquired about live-aboard dive boats, but the boat operators said they didn't specifically go to my island and that if I wanted to make a special stop, I'd have to hire the entire boat for a ten-day cruise.

Then I heard about Misool Eco-Resort, a new dive-oriented hotel just an hour from the object of my quest.

With Marit Miners, one of the resort directors, I visited Fanfalap, a village of 200 that has jurisdiction over part of the region. "Nope, our control doesn't include your island," Ahmad, the head of the village, patiently explained. "And no, we have no idea why it's called by that odd name."

But I had the coordinates, and Marit organized a group dive to the island.

We got out the GPS and approached. But the CIA in its wisdom only listed the location to the minute, not to the second. Our boat arrived at the CIA coordinates. We were in the middle of the dark azure sea, about half a kilometer equidistant between two islands. The island to the north was the large and well-known Pulau Daram. The smaller, idyllic-appearing island to the south, about 200 meters (a quarter mile) long, I decided was my oceanic grail.

To celebrate, I dived into the water and was startled, then pleased, to see a hawksbill turtle swim by. It wasn't too large, about the size of a jumbo pizza. Turtles can be just turtles, but they can also be omens and cosmic messengers, and in my semi-sun-burned state I chose to believe that this reptile was gliding around for a purpose.

As I was swimming, I thought that maybe the CIA-indicated location was correct, but the island was invisible, a covert CIA installation hidden deep below the surface, like a secret redoubt of a villain in a James Bond movie. After all, it was the all-knowing CIA that provided the coordinates.

We went ashore, and my island (by now I had become more than a little protective of it) was a delight, with three white sand beaches and palms. A fisherman was on the beach, taking a break, and I asked him what the name of the island was. "Pulau Pinang," he said, referring to the name of a common palm tree. And where was Pulau Valse Pisang? "Oh, that's far away. Really far."

Never mind. I had made an executive decision that this island was the one, and I was happy. But just for a while.

Then I had another thought, triggered by the earlier sighting of the constantly questing turtle.

Perhaps my Pulau Valse Pisang island is transient and therefore everywhere but nowhere. Sort of like an itinerant jester deity that enjoys creating geographical conundrums — an oceanic Brigadoon.

Indonesian culture and belief systems are what the anthropologists call syncretic. In a huge over-simplification, ancient Indonesians started with various forms of Animism and mysticism, then, like a hoarder, they didn't throw anything away. The accumulative Indonesians added layers of Vedic traditions, then Hindu, then Buddhist, then Muslim, even notions of Christianity and the modern religions of nation-building, celebrity-worship, consumerism, and social media. From my viewpoint, the Hindu tradition is one of the most interesting. Hindu mythology recognizes Kurma, the second avatar of Vishnu, a celestial turtle that played an invaluable role in churning the Sea of Milk to produce the nectar of immortality (it's complicated). Perhaps my Dancing Banana Island continually swims the oceans on its sacred turtle, gracefully waving its flippers in three-quarters time.

The God Who Flew Off With a Mountain

It Takes Chutzpah for an Indian Villager to Stay Angry at One of the Most Popular Gods in the Hindu Pantheon, But Padhan Patti Wants Her Mountain Back

Paul Spencer Sochaczewski

What kind of a god abandons Auntie in a blizzard?

DUNAGIRI, INDIA

*I*t takes a great glob of Hindu courage for a remote Indian villager to stay angry at one of the most popular gods in the pantheon, but Padhan Patti feels she has a good reason.

"When Lord Hanuman came here to retrieve the medicinal plant mountain, he promised to bring it back," the 50-something

5

woman says, referring to a pivotal scene in the classic *Ramayana* epic. "But he didn't." Padhan Patti promises that when I hike another few hours to a vantage point, I will see a huge red scar on the side of Dunagiri Mountain where the flying monkey god Hanuman is said to have sliced off a big chunk of mythological real estate, a scar that "bleeds" in the afternoon sun.

Padhan Patti says she still respects Hanuman, the flying monkey god, because after all he is the Hindu epitome of devotion, selfless courage, and good works. Nevertheless, to register her disappointment in his lapse to keep his word, she refuses to take the *prasad*, or communion, at the village's annual Hanuman festival.

But it's even more intriguing that Patti's family, and three other families in this remote, high-altitude summer village of just a few hundred people, would bear a grudge for a slight that originated 880,000 years ago, which, according to some Vedic scholars, is the time when the Ramayana action took place.

⸻◆⸻

Having immense religious and cultural influence, with some of the story lines and poetry of the *Bible*, the *Odyssey*, the *Ring* cycle, and the search for the Holy Grail, the *Ramayana* is a hero's journey involving palace intrigue, broken families, fierce *Star Wars*-like battles with a grand collection of deities, ogres and demons, and ultimately the triumph of good over evil. In the story, Prince Rama (an avatar of Vishnu, one of the most powerful Hindu deities) is exiled by his stepmother so her biological son can take the throne. Rama, accompanied by his wife, Sita, and his brother, Lakshmana, wander the Indian forests. Sita is kidnapped by the ten-headed demon-king Ravana, who spirits the woman to his well-protected redoubt in the mythical kingdom of Lanka (thought to be located in what is now Sri Lanka). During the numerous battles to rescue Sita, Lakshmana is mortally wounded. The only thing that can save him is *sanjivani*, a combination of medicinal plants that only grow in the high Himalaya. The royal physician bemoans: "But we're stuck here in Lanka, and the plants grow near the border with Tibet.

Who we gonna call?"

This is when Hanuman comes to the rescue. The monkey god flies north some 2,600 kilometers (1,600 miles) to the medicinal plant mountain, soaring at a speed of roughly 660 kilometers an hour (about 410 miles per hour), according to Robert P. Goldman, from the University of California at Berkeley, who made his calculation based on the writings of ancient scholars. And then, depending on which of the many versions of the story you read, Hanuman either forgets which plants were on the shopping list or the plants hide in fear when they see this big monkey coming in for a landing. Either way, he rips up the mountain and carries it back to Lanka. After one whiff of the healing herbs, Lakshmana is back in business, and Rama and his brother win the final battle, rescue Sita, and return home for a bittersweet finale. Importantly, at least for this quest, in most versions of the story, after the medicines have worked their magic, Hanuman puts the mountain back on his shoulder and flies again over the subcontinent to replace the mountain in its rightful place.

⚬———◆———⚬

I was both exhausted and thrilled as we trudged up the steep, narrow path to Dunagiri village. I've wanted to find Hanuman's mountain for some 30 years. Partly it was the quest for something that is inherently "unfindable," but I was also intrigued by an unintended side benefit. It is difficult to fly over a subcontinent carrying a mountain like a pizza delivery guy without bits of it falling to the ground. Where these clumps of medicinal-plant dirt fell, sacred forests sprouted. These holy groves, places rich in medicinal plants and generally protected by the local communities, can be found throughout Asia (and indeed throughout the world). During my work in nature conservation, I took a particular interest in their existence and the practical, cultural and spiritual benefits such natural gardens provide to local people. How interesting it would be, I thought, to find the mother lode of these sacred forests.

⚬———◆———⚬

But where was it? I read dozens of books and spoke to a gaggle of scholars. One *Ramayana* version said: "Go over the sea and north into the far high Himalaya. At night, from the air, you will easily see the glowing Medicine Hill of Life, crowned with herbs long ago transplanted from the Moon." Another translation of the *Ramayana* places the medicinal-plant mountain between the (mythical) Rishabha mountain, full of fierce animals, and the (very real) Kailasa mountain in Tibet. Yet another instructs Hanuman to fly 9,000 *yojanas* to the red mountain, then another 9,000 yojanas to the blue mountain, and on and on (Indian scholars estimate that one ancient yojana is equal to approximately 13 to 16 kilometers — eight to 10 miles). N.C. Shah, of the Central Council for Research in Indian Medicine in Lucknow, pointed me toward Dunagiri by noting that Hanuman's mountain was located "where *kshir*, or ocean, was churned for *amrita*, ambrosia, and where existed two hills, namely Chandra and Drona." An Indian conservation official said no, the mountain is in his home state of Tamil Nadu, in the south of the country. More prosaically, a friend in Mumbai asked "Why are you interested in this goose chase in the first place? No shopping malls in the mountains."

Eventually, Ajay Rastogi, a friend in Delhi with whom I had worked during my tenure at the World Wide Fund for Nature, said that he had heard about a mountain village where some folks refused to share in Hanuman's communion. Ajay couldn't make the trip, but he introduced me to Gopal Sharma, a tough Indian mountaineer and adventurer. Gopal had twice summited 7,817-meter (25,600 feet) Nanda Devi. In one climb he survived a night bivouac without a sleeping bag at 7,600 meters (19,800 feet), and on another attempt he survived a 400-meter (13,000-foot) fall.

After a comfortable overnight train from Delhi to Haridwar, a holy city where the Ganges leaves the mountains and enters the plains, Gopal and I drove 12 hours to Joshimath, an Indian hill station in the state of Uttaranchal (now Uttarakhand) that suffers from the ugly unregulated construction and traffic of most such Indian resorts. The next morning, driving toward the border with China, we drove another two hours to the trailhead, altitude 2,578 meters

(8,500 feet), in the general vicinity of the Nanda Devi National Park.

I slowly climbed to our campsite at Dunagiri village at 3,651 meters (12,000 feet).

This was ground zero for my search. The hundred or so villagers in Dunagiri (the village, and the mountain of the same name, are sometimes referred to as Dronagiri) were curious, polite, and after a while willing to answer the strange questions of an out-of-breath foreigner. You can't see the 7,066-meter (23,182 foot) Dunagiri mountain from the village, so Gopal and I hiked up a few hundred meters to get a good view. We were lucky with the weather; the snow-topped mountain shone like a beacon. We clearly saw the gash where part of the mountain had been sliced off. Near our lunchtime picnic spot in the meadows, we found one of the medicinal plants on Hanuman's shopping list, *visalyakarani*, which in Sanskrit means "removing spikes and arrows." G.S. Rawat of the Wildlife Institute of India subsequently identified the plant as *Morina longifolia* (Dipsacaceae), used locally to heal wounds.

⋯⋯◆⋯⋯

Like many myths, the search for healing plants in the Himalaya has a basis in reality. Scientists and local people alike know well that the Himalayan region is a treasure chest of important medicinal plants that form the heart of the Ayurvedic system of medicine used to treat Lakshmana, and which remains the medical system of choice for tens of millions of Indians, Nepalese, and Sri Lankans.

⋯⋯◆⋯⋯

We returned to the village to say goodbye. I wanted to be clear that I had the story right and asked Padhan Patti to confirm that she really was upset with Hanuman because he hadn't returned the mountain. She nodded, but added a new fillip, another reason for being angry. She told the story with a familiarity and acceptance, as if she was recounting a family tale that happened, say, a generation ago, like my father's war stories. "Hanuman flew in during a white-out," she said, "and couldn't find the mountain. The only person in the village was an old woman." Padhan Patti's voice took on a surprising hardness: "That was my Auntie. She explained that Hanuman-ji said he couldn't see it, and he was in a hurry. Hanuman told Auntie he didn't have time to fly around looking for a mountain, so he put her on his shoulder to navigate. When they arrived at the peak, Hanuman placed Auntie on the ground, ripped off a chunk of the mountain and flew away."

"And then what happened," I asked.

"Hanuman left Auntie alone in the wilderness in the middle of a blizzard."

In Search of...
ROOTS

AUNT SARAH RATHER LIKED HER ORIGINAL CHILDHOOD NAME

Popping Balloons Instead of Chinese Firecrackers in the Hawaiian Melting Pot

Sochaczewski Family Archives c. 1915   *Sochaczewski Family Archives c. 1928*

(Left) Sarah Sochaczewski, age about five, when she was
told to change her name in order to enroll in school.
(Right) Sarah, now calling herself Syd, age about 18.

HONOLULU, HAWAI'I

I filled out the forms and wished my ancestors had been Burmese or Chinese. I was changing my name to my grandfather's original and Win or Wong would have been a lot easier to put on a new credit card than Sochaczewski.

But we have little control over whose descendants we are. My grandfather Josef Sochaczewski came to America from Kalisz, Poland, then part of Russia, in 1912 as part of the great wave of European immigration. His family — my grandmother Esther, my

13

father Samuel, and my aunt, whom I always called Syd — followed in 1913. In an old family portrait, taken around 1915 (above, left), my mustached grandfather looks like a proud Polish Pavarotti. My grandmother, pregnant with my uncle Bill, resembles a weary but very wise Madonna. She had tuberculosis when the photo was taken and died a year later.

After passing through immigration at Ellis Island, the family lived with my grandfather's sister, Lena, and her family, in Hoboken, New Jersey. It soon came time for the young girl to go to school. Her Aunt Lena, the only relative who spoke English well, accompanied the girl. But the school official, apparently aghast at such an odd and difficult name as Sochaczewski, refused to register her and told Lena to come back with a simpler moniker for the girl. Today, the school official's politically incorrect action would be grounds for dismissal (if not a lawsuit); around 1915, he had simply made my family an offer they couldn't refuse. Aunt Lena, thinking quickly, suggested that her niece be registered instead as Wachtel, which was Lena's married name.

My grandfather thought this was fine, since, to him, the German name Wachtel sounded more American than the Polish Sochacze-wski. Like most immigrants of that period, he wanted to jump into the American melting pot as quickly as possible, so he legally changed the family name to Wachtel.

⸻◆⸻

Americans change their names for many reasons. Some are moti-vated by show business glitter (Norma Jeane Mortenson, later Baker, to Marilyn Monroe), some by religious conviction (Cassius Marcellus Clay Jr. to Muhammad Ali), and some by a personal vision of how a commercially successful name is constructed (John Paul "Jack" Rosenberg to the personal development guru, Werner Erhard).

But most name-changers of the early 20th century, like my grand-father, never made the limelight. Thousands of people strove to de-link from their pasts. It seems this desire to become American (and by definition un-become Italian or Russian or Polish) was part of a ritual cleansing, a symbolic burning of old *vêtements*, as if to say, "I can't, I won't go home again."

As I grew older, I realized that home is comprised of many nests. I was at a point where my life was in transition. For me, the way forward lay in a desire to return to roots. I wanted to change my name, and while I had known the story of my family's name change for years, several factors had prevented me from reverting to the original.

The first was concern that my modest writing career would be hindered. The second was that I dreaded having to change all my records. And the third was that, as an American expatriate in Switzerland, I had to wait until I returned to the United States long enough to establish a legal residence in America, which was required for a formal name change.

The fourth problem, however, was the most serious. No one in our family knew how to spell the original name.

I played with different spellings, even going so far as to send some orthographic variants to a numerologist friend in India who calculated the relative impact of different phonetic spellings of what I thought my name might be.

I eventually went to the Ellis Island Museum and saw an exhibit of belongings immigrants had brought with them to America. The handmade doll in a display case was probably not much different from a similar cuddly-friend I imagine Aunt Syd caressing; the stuffed bear similar, perhaps, to one my father might have embraced. I saw women's jewelry and men's watches and photos and mementos of home that were lightweight enough to fit into a steamer trunk but heavy enough to provide solace during the uncertain future. I admired the courage these people had to leave for a place where they neither spoke the language nor had any guarantee of success. I have lived overseas for more than half my life, but my adventures seem smaller than those of my daring relatives.

Officials at Ellis Island put me in touch with the National Archives and Records Administration in Bayonne, New Jersey. I told them what I had been heard about the family's arrival in America. Several weeks later they sent me photocopies as long as my arm of the original folio pages from passengers arriving in Ellis Island aboard the SS Kaiserin Auguste Victoria, sailing from Hamburg. It was the best use of the taxpayers' money that I've come across. SOCHACZEWSKI, the folio said. I called up some Polish friends to learn how to pronounce it (say: soh-kha-CHEV-ski). I practiced my signature a few times (it still hurts my hand to write it, and I'm not comfortable enough with it yet to scrawl it). I spelled it on the phone to friends, first in English, then in French. It felt like I had been dealt a Scrabble hand with no vowels.

I took a sabbatical at the East-West Center in Honolulu, and the office of the Lieutenant Governor, Benjamin Cayetano, was helpful in walking me through the name-change paperwork. Most Americans are immigrants, of course, but it felt somehow suitable to go back to my Polish roots in the Hawaiian melting pot. Fannie, the Chinese-American woman in the East-West Center in charge of aloha (that's her real job description), organized a quasi-Chinese ceremony — in politically correct and safety-conscious Hawai'i we substituted bursting balloons for firecrackers.

I changed my name, not so much because I feel Polish (I don't speak a word of it) but because I don't feel German (and I certainly don't feel like a quail, which is how Wachtel translates). Somehow it feels right. The 19th-century Scottish philosopher, Thomas Carlyle, recognized that a name can shape a life, reflecting "…what mystic influence does it not send inwards, even to the centre."

Almost as cosmic proof that I chose wisely, surprising and pleasant coincidences began. Strangers see my complicated name in a publication and write to me, asking if, just possibly, we might be related. A newly found cousin in Montreal, Ari Sochaczewski, invited me to his son's bar mitzvah. I told a friend in Basel, Switzerland, about the name change, and she explained that she had a friend, Simon Sochaczewski, also in Basel, with a similar name. We couldn't possibly be related, I thought, but she spelled his name, and it had the same odd concurrence of Slavic consonants. I called him, learned about his service in the Résistance in France. He mentioned a relative who had moved to Brooklyn. "I'm from Brooklyn!" I said and immediately called Aunt Syd. "Sure, Jack Sachs," she remembered, explaining that Simon's/Jack's branch of the family Anglicized the name rather than changing it completely, as ours had done. "Jack died about twenty years ago." I called Simon back, and we figured out that we are second cousins, I think (I'm not very good at figuring out these family trees). Right here in Switzerland.

When I first decided to make the name change, I called my aunt, who started all this trouble by wanting to go to school some four-score years ago.

She calls herself Syd, and I asked her why. "My name was Sadie," she explained, "but I never liked that name, so I changed it to Syd."

"But your name isn't Sadie," I said. "It's Sarah. Says so right here on the immigration documents they filled out when you got off the boat at Ellis Island. *Name:* Sarah. *Age:* Four years old. *Nationality:* Russian. *Race:* Jewish. *Final destination:* Brooklyn. It says here you were 'illiterate.'"

"Oh my," my 80-something Aunt Syd/Sarah replied. "If I had known that, I never would have changed my name. I rather like the name Sarah, don't you?"

Uncle Joe and Aunt Anisoara
Dreaming Greenwich Village Eccentric
Meets Truth-Bending
Transylvanian Sentimentalist

Samuel Wachtel

Anisoara and Joe at their Stony Creek, New York, house, c. 1950.

CLUJ, TRANSYLVANIA, ROMANIA, AND GREENWICH VILLAGE, NEW YORK

*M*y uncle and aunt's love affair illustrates the challenges of trying to decipher a relationship.

How could I not love an uncle who, when he babysat me, let me stay up well past my bedtime to watch wrestling (Antonino Rocca was my favorite) and horror movies (Boris Karloff's *The Mummy* was the scariest)? How could I not love an uncle who lived in the middle of Greenwich Village, who took me to my first Broadway show, who tried to disprove Einstein? How could I not love an uncle who invented a slew of innovative gadgets, and who chastised major

19

corporations for their lousy ad campaigns — and then offered them new campaigns that were hardly better? How could I not love an uncle who married a wannabe Romanian noble and bought a farm in the middle of the Adirondack mountains because it resembled his wife's native Transylvania?

Uncle Joe Rubin died of colon cancer in 1960 when I was 13. I was at an age when I was particularly incurious about life's complexities and more than a little spooked by having a close family member wither away in our spare room.

Why is it that we neglect to ask the good questions when the opportunities arise?

Joe was my mother's older brother. He was a gentle and generous soul. He nurtured me and took me into New York City to attend the theater, to eat in real restaurants, the ones with tablecloths. I loved it when he would babysit — he would defy my parent's bedtime instructions, and together we would stay up late and eat ice cream. He was a Bohemian — after serving in the Navy in World War II, he lived smack in the middle of Greenwich Village — Barrow Street — at the time one of the intellectual hubs of America. He married a head-strong but sentimental Transylvanian, Anisoara Stan, a romance that no doubt caused raised eyebrows in both families.

I wonder if Joe was disappointed that I wasn't a child prodigy, that I was just an acned adolescent who didn't fully appreciate the brave new worlds he was willing to show me.

How marvelous and intriguing are the secrets of relatives now gone. What genes of theirs do I have? What would I say to them if they were around today, and we could speak adult-to-adult? Would I find Joe to be a charming and well-read companion? Or an eccentric dreamer just a few steps away from sitting on a park bench feeding pigeons?

Is there absolute truth?

A classic exercise used by law school professors introducing first-year students to the legal profession works like this: While the professor is making her opening remarks, a man rushes on stage, wielding a gun. A shouting woman runs after him, followed by police, bystanders, innocent children, and multiple bad guys. Shots are fired, people are wounded (spurting blood!), screams are heard, entreaties are shouted. The action is played by student actors, who, after a minute of mayhem, run out of the classroom. The professor then asks her students "What just happened?" And not one student gets the story right. *How many shots? How many people with weapons? What clothes did the shooter wear? What words were spoken? How many were injured?* "That's the job of a lawyer," the teacher says. "Out of confusion you have to put your own spin on reality." The teacher might have added that "fabricating truth" is also the job of the historian.

Anisoara died in 1954 when I was just seven. I hardly knew her; if I can dredge my memories (and who knows whether they are accurate), Anisoara was a sturdy and strange woman who wore unusual clothes and cooked weird food. Probably, if I had known her as an adult, I might have been drawn to her as an elegant, eccentric, cosmopolitan artist. A dreamer. A truth-bender. My kind of people.

But I was a child. I was taken to her funeral, which was held in an Eastern Orthodox church in Manhattan. My only vague memory is of getting nauseous from the incense and the overbearing otherworldly chanting. My mother had to take me out of the church before I vomited on the other mourners.

So basically, I have no memory of her.

What I do have is a written record. Her 1947 autobiography *They Crossed Mountains and Oceans* ($3.75 hardback). Her 1951 gastro-autobiography, *The Romanian Cookbook* ($3). A number of her letters. The eulogy Uncle Joe gave at her funeral. This is far more documentation than I have for my parents.

So, based on Anisoara's autobiography, written when she was 48 and living with Joe in Greenwich Village, I know the following:

- She was from a good, perhaps noble, family from Cluj, Transylvania.
- She was a protégé of Queen Marie of Romania (Queen Victoria's granddaughter).
- Queen Marie sent Anisoara to the States to promote Romanian culture, which she did with energy but mixed success.
- While in the States, she became a favorite of the intellectual/diplomatic communities. (Harold Stassen, governor of Minnesota and nine-time Republican presidential candidate, was a reliable supporter).
- She promoted the glory of the Romanian peasant and liked to wear peasant clothing.
- She had tea with Eleanor Roosevelt, who later attended one of Anisoara's art exhibitions.
- She gave Mrs. Roosevelt a Romanian peasant dress, which the First Lady wore to a White House ball.
- She had a dream to set up the World Village of Peasant Art, which would showcase the colorful folk legends, customs, and handicrafts of ethnic groups from around the world. Her objective: peace and love, Yoko Ono style.
- She was a poor writer.
- She and Joe had no children.

So, there it is, her life reduced to a few "facts."

As it turns out, the above list is a combination of truth, opinion (trust me, she was a poor writer), and exaggeration. Her version of her life is riddled with speculation, embellishments, and mis-remembering. She presented alternative facts. Enhanced reality. Thoughtful balderdash. Or to be less charitable, Anisoara lied. And I don't blame her. We all lie when we tell our personal stories.

Memory is a tricky, unreliable resource.

Put simply, we all fib. Sometimes intentionally. Sometimes we forget things. Most often we skew the truth because we filter experiences through our own points of view. The film *Rashomon* explains how the same event will always be interpreted differently depending on who is telling the story.

Most of life's background noise, found in day-to-day gossip, reports, memoirs, and chatter is merely foggy obfuscation, a cacophony of smoke and mirrors.

And the more we repeat a story, the truer it becomes. Psychologists call this the "illusory truth effect." Say something frequently, with enough conviction, and the concept becomes embedded like quick-drying cement. And, in turn, the more you repeat something (hello "fake news"), the greater the chance the audience will accept your words as true. A related concept familiar to psychologists and political strategists is the term "confirmation bias." Elizabeth Kolbert, writing in *The New Yorker*, describes this as "the tendency people have to embrace information that supports their beliefs and reject information that contradicts them." Or, as noted physicist Richard Feynman put it: "The first principle is that you must not fool yourself — and you are the easiest person to fool."

I went to Transylvania to see if I could learn more about Anisoara's life.

Once again, thank you to Tim Berners-Lee for inventing the internet. I found a site that lists private guides worldwide, and singled out a handful of possible individuals in Transylvania who might have been able to help in my quest. I corresponded with them and found one woman, Geta, who seemed to understand and appreciate that I wasn't a normal tourist who wanted to see Dracula's castle. When she picked me up at the airport, she said "I can help you, but you really should talk to my brother. I told him about your journey, and he has some ideas." So I had dinner with her and her brother, Iosif (Joseph in Romanian, a happy coincidence), and we agreed that Iosif would take charge of me for a few days.

Iosif is a good teacher, which makes him a good student. He's curious and energetic — one summer he went to Portugal and worked on an isolated farm. He explained that he already knew the languages of the far east of Europe and thought that as a modern European he should similarly learn the languages of the far west.

What makes Iosif such an impressive historian is that he can interpret "factual" statements for historical accuracy as well as for political and social nuance.

We visited places Anisoara mentioned in her books, and he dissected Anisoara's life story with the determination and skill of a physicist at CERN trying to figure out how to detect a Higgs boson. Iosif decided that "unravelling her deliberate exaggerations would be the key to deciphering Anisoara's autobiography."

He even took the time to write a 40-page analysis of Anisoara's life, filtered through his knowledge of history, politics, and instinct. He noted dozens of anomalies, many dealing with Anisoara's ancestors' peasant roots, and her political aspirations. Based on details, such as the large open fireplace in her parents' brick home, the fact that they raised chickens and cows, and other details — he concluded that she was one generation removed from a simple rural existence.

Iosif said, "Her parents were likely born in a poor environment, perhaps peasants, but rose in status. They were educated and lived well in turn-of-the-century Cluj, then part of the Austro-Hungarian empire. They had well-placed friends. Her family was not noble, but perhaps they wanted to be. One might call them *arrivistes*. As a result, Anisoara grew up in a rich, powerful, and locally prestigious bourgeois family."

These are biographical facts, admittedly, as suggested by Iosif. But behind the facts lies a more nuanced story of how she manipulated details to promote a political agenda that glorified the Transylvanian peasant.

Anisoara grew up in Transylvania, in the north. But in her books, she claims to remember performing dances that came from the south and would have been unknown to her. In her dust-jacket photo she wears a costume she implies is Transylvanian, but which actually comes from southern Romania. But for her, accuracy was subservient to political correctness, since that type of dress was worn by Queen Marie to show solidarity with the peasants and earn their political support.

Iosif was clear about Romanian Peasant Politics: "The early twentieth-century rulers of the country needed the peasants (who formed more than 80 percent of the population) to obey and join the emerging nationalistic movement. But at the same time the leaders needed those peasants to feel proud enough of themselves so that they would obey the leaders without having the sentiment that they *must* obey.

"Then, just after the end of the First World War, when north-of-the-Carpathians Transylvanians (closer to Budapest and the moral authority of Rome) were uniting with south-of-the-Carpathians Romanians (with affinities to the dying Ottoman Empire), Anisoara and her family "switched sides" and became ardent nationalists — Anisoara was briefly imprisoned during the early days of this political changeover. And part of that nationalistic discourse, eagerly adopted by Anisoara, was the idealization of the noble, hard-working, artistic Romanian peasant."

On the surface, her two books are prose Hallmark cards about Romanian culture and the goodness of the peasants. In her cookbook, she gushed: "With such tasty food, it is little wonder that the Romanian peasants are so healthy ... Good food puts one in a happy state of mind, the body becomes relaxed and the digestion improved. But equally important is their attitude towards life, a love of the soil and of nature's work, their songs and dances, their fairy tales related to the children ... their famous evenings where the spinning and weaving takes on a festive air, their embroidery and carpet weaving, the making of the peasant costumes, the painting on pottery, and even the painstaking carvings on their wooden household utensils. All this gives them no time to feel bored. They are busy and happy."

But her peasant adoration also had a political purpose.

In America, she tried to serve several cultural masters. She wrote her two books, no doubt, partly to enhance her position as an independent-thinking émigré American while not putting her Romanian family in jeopardy back home by the increasingly autocratic governments. (In 1938, Romania started to be governed by a long chain of dictatorships that lasted 51 years).

And she hoped her books would promote a Romanian national identity that gave her a calling card in America that would enhance her credibility with potential donors for her proposed museum of peasant art.

Her biggest fib, however, revolved around her purported relationship with Queen Marie of Romania and the reasons she went to America.

Throughout the book, Anisoara implies that Queen Marie sent her to America in 1922 as an unofficial ambassador to promote Romanian culture and values at a time when the country was striving for international recognition.

But that seems to be a big fib, loaded with unanswered questions.

She writes that she met Queen Marie at a public reception in Cluj in 1919 during the royal family's first visit to Transylvania, following which the Queen invited her for a private chat the same evening. She met Queen Marie a second time in 1922 at a reception at the royal palace in Bucharest, shortly after Anisoara got her first passport.

She implies that the Queen gave her letters of introduction.

She implies that the Queen appointed her as ambassador.

"Grossly fictionalized," is Iosif's conclusion.

For a start, Anisoara was just 23 when she went to America, accompanied by her younger sister Flora and cousin Letitia. Anisoara had gone to a good school, had worked for high-level government officials, perhaps as a secretary, and had well-placed friends. But she was 23. She no doubt knew Romanian, Hungarian, French, and probably some German and a little English. She had never been out of her country; in fact, she had never been out of Transylvania until she went to Bucharest to get a passport (where she was surprised to learn that the southern Romanians had a baksheesh culture). She had virtually no contact with people outside her immediate circle. Did she have the profile of an ambassador? Certainly not. Did she do a good job anyway? Absolutely. I feel that she was a gutsy, smart, ambitious (and cunning) woman.

Look at the discrepancies. She was a travel virgin. She had no higher education and zero diplomatic experience. If she had been the envoy of Queen Marie, she wouldn't have had to go all the way to Bucharest to get a passport (nor had to negotiate with the corrupt government servants in the passport office). She would have been given funds for the sea voyage, instead of having to ask her mother for the money. She wouldn't have had to sleep on the couches of working-class Transylvanians in America. She would have had some "official" money, instead of being nearly broke during her early years — in one emotional scene Anisoara writes that she and her sister were staying in a cheap hotel in New York and running out of money. Her sister Flora revealed that she had some extra money (gold coins?) sewn into her dress to use in an emergency. And, most important, if she had been a true protégé of Queen Marie, Anisoara would have had the full support of Romanian diplomats in America. In fact, she was actively rebuffed by most of the diplomats whom she asked for support. Numerous times in her autobiography she recalls that her valiant energies and events were accomplished *in spite of* obstructions by Romanian officials.

⌁────◆────⌁

Anisoara implies that she went to America to find better economic conditions. But Iosif notes "in my opinion, Anisoara hides something. It seems to me that it is highly probable that her first flirtations with the idea of going to America were triggered not only by economic necessities but also by some political purposes; she might have wanted to do something extraordinary in America to enhance the status of her family on the Romanian political scene at a time when there was such political confusion."

The confusion assumed divergent aspects. One side of the political discourse was fiercely nationalistic, fueled by the late 19th-century poetry of Mihai Eminescu, the last great romantic poet in Europe. But in opposition, the old elite clung to an idea of Romantic dandyism — duels of honor were not unknown, and men were instructed, from French literary references, in the 30 ways to shape a moustache.

On December 1, 1918, the province of Transylvania united with the Old Kingdom.

Anisoara's family walked a geopolitical tightrope of political alliances, and part of Anisoara's unofficial mission to America no doubt involved lobbying Transylvanian expatriates to support one group or another. But her motives and ultimate goals are unclear. Iosif lists the possibilities: Perhaps she went to the States to persuade the large Romanian-Transylvanian diaspora (between 1890 to 1914, some 200,000 Romanian Transylvanians went to the States) to continue to support the Austro-Hungarian Habsburgs (even though the last Habsburg emperor, Charles I, "renounced participation" in state affairs in 1922). Or her goal might have been to support a rebellious Transylvanian independence movement. But maybe she wanted to support a more politically correct union of Transylvania with Greater Romania. I recall the Chinese curse: "May you live in interesting times."

———◆———

Queen Marie, who refused an offer of marriage to her cousin, the future King George V of England, was herself a political animal.

Queen Marie knew how to play the game of strategic marriages, a dance that has always been an entertaining part of European history. Her daughter Elisabeth became Queen of Greece, her daughter Maria became Queen of Yugoslavia, and her daughter Ileana, whom everyone expected to marry the future king of Bulgaria, surprised observers and married the Archduke of Austria. They were a cosmopolitan lot, comfortable speaking English, German, Romanian, and French. One can only imagine the royal gossip they exchanged (in what language, one wonders?) around the dinner table.

But no doubt part of her drive was to improve the image and credibility of Romania in America.

Uncle Joe remembered that at the time "Romania had an extremely bad press in America. It was considered to be either a musical comedy country [due to the antics of Marie's son King Carol and the salacious stories about Queen Marie herself] or anti-democratic. *Life* magazine said that Romanians were 'hot blooded gypsies.' Anisoara realized that it was essential for a small nation like Romania to make real friends of a powerful country like the USA."

Josiah Brill, a lawyer in Minnesota with whom Anisoara worked on the World Peasant Art project, wrote: "She is a crusader, just like Mme. Curie."

⟡

Anisoara sailed to America laden with trunks containing peasant dresses, handicrafts, carvings, paintings, embroidery and carpets, tablecloths, and head scarves, Orthodox icons, and jewelry. These objects were her tools of the trade as unofficial cultural ambassador. (They likely were also her dowry.) With these items and other costumes and crafts she collected from Transylvanian émigrés in the States, Anisoara staged exhibitions throughout the country, culminating in a large and successful show at the Shoreham Hotel in Washington, DC. This event was a turning point — Eleanor Roosevelt attended the exposition and not only bought one of the Transylvanian peasant dresses on display but wore it to a state dinner, an achievement for Anisoara that she proudly told and retold.

When Anisoara died, Joe donated her folk art collection to St. Mary's cathedral in Cleveland, Ohio, where it still is displayed.

I have one physical memento of her, a hand-carved wooden box, decorated in an exuberant style.

I have just one physical object that belonged to Joe — his slide rule, constructed of wood and Bakelite, and made by "Keuffel & Esser Co. New York," with a patent notice for "June 5, 1909." It's in a battered brown leather case on which he had etched in pen a monogram with his initials. (Yes, I know how to use it for simple multiplication and division.) Similar pieces can be bought on eBay for around $20. And I have numerous photos. In one picture he appears in military uniform, wearing a state trooper-style wide-brimmed hat, standing stiffly at attention with his rifle by his side. In another he stands on the steps of what could be a government building or a school. He reminds me of a between-the-wars spy, or lawyer, or businessman. Hard to tell.

⸺◆⸺

Every Romeo needs a Juliet. Every artist needs a muse. Every hero in an adventure movie relies on a sidekick.

So it was with Joe and Anisoara. He needed her; she needed him.

⸺◆⸺

When they first met, Anisoara was smitten. Sounding like a teenager writing in her diary, Anisoara later wrote in her autobiography: "God brought me a prince charming, a young man who smiled so devilishly not only with his whole face but his eyes as well and who had what we call *vino incoace* — a 'come here' look. Was it love at first sight? Yes, yes, it was. We met [perhaps at Joe's sister Jeanne's home in Bedford Hills, New York] on Decoration Day, May 30, and spoke only a few words."

Joe apparently felt the same. In his eulogy of Anisoara he said: "I saw her for an instant, and in that brief moment, knew no other girl could ever exist for me. She had outer beauty, of course, but it was her inner beauty that captivated me. In our first conversation, I realized I was speaking to one of the few chosen people of the earth, and with the years, this feeling has grown and grown."

Anisoara continued her retelling of Joe's courtship. "Before he said goodbye, he asked for my name and address." She played hard to get and told him: "What for? I do not see any reason for it. I am leaving the United States on my return to the city. I am glad I met you, but no name, no address. Goodbye."

According to Anisoara, Joe replied: "Just one word. When do

you leave for Europe?"

"Thirteenth of September."

"Oh, that's fine," Joe said. "You will hear from me."

And she did, writing: "After a few days I got a note from him with a little pressed violet enclosed." Joe's missive said: "Hello, Ann — I am at my sister's [Jeanne's] country place in Bedford Hills. Found this in the garden and, as I thought of you, I am sending it along. Won't you please write just a few words?"

But Anisoara continued to be aloof. "No, and I didn't [write back]. But how did he find my name? Oh, well, I won't think of him. Funny, I didn't even know his name … After a few days, a small package arrived. It was a book in leather binding in my favorite color, dark red wine. It was *A Pair of Blue Eyes*, by Thomas Hardy, with a neat inscription, 'To Anna, the most beautiful girl I ever met. From Joe, June 2, 1930.'"

So, here's the dating conundrum. Anisoara (Ann, or Anna, to Joe) didn't want to get involved. Nevertheless, she confessed: "I feel so funny inside of me about this fine American with his so humane eyes and that characteristic smile of his, which causes little wrinkles at the corners … and his so handsome dark oval face."

She liked his style: "He wore his clothes nonchalantly, in a devil may care way."

And what might have sealed the deal was the Thomas Hardy book, which she loved.

But Anisoara was no stranger to being courted. She wasn't a seductress in the modern sense, but she had an energy that some men appreciated. She recalled that she had almost been engaged to a millionaire, a half-American, half-English man, living in South America who wrote to her parents asking for her hand. Anisoara's mother wrote to her daughter that although he was no doubt rich and good-looking, "you don't love that man, you are just attracted to him. Don't do it." And Anisoara didn't.

And so it went. Joe persisted, Anisoara resisted. He called and sent her letters; she refused all contact. A lesser man would have given up.

Finally, she agreed to have dinner with him at Enrico & Paglieri, a noted (and now defunct) Italian restaurant in Greenwich Village, with her sister Flora as chaperone.

The following morning after their dinner, Joe visited her again and asked her to marry him.

She said "No, I'm going home in six days."

"All right," Joe said. "Marry me and then you can go."

Anisoara was conflicted. "I saw him only three times, and yet I don't give a hoot about anything (as you Americans say) but him. But I refused again. I told him, 'First I must go back home. Let this be our secret engagement. I'll come back.'"

But Joe was both determined and a deal-maker. "No," she said he said. "Either you marry me now, and I'll be sure of you, or I will not marry you at all."

She agreed. They were married on Saturday, September 13, 1930, the day she had earlier told him she was leaving.

Anisoara then went to Romania for a year. On her return, Joe said he would support her work to promote Romanian folk art. He agreed she could use her maiden name.

Yet in her 1936 US passport ("not valid for travel to Spain") and her 1948 US passport ("invalid for Germany, Austria, Japan, Korea, and Yugoslavia"), she used Joe's family name: Anna Rubin.

<hr>

One dream occupied Anisoara more than any other.

I went through her papers and found notes and proposals for her grand project, which she alternatively called the Outdoor Museum of Villages of All Peoples, the World Village of Peasant Art, the Ethnographic Museum of Peasant Art and (in the hope she could gain UN recognition), the United Nations Ethnographic Museum. She wrote dozens of letters to ambassadors and high-ranking officials requesting support, and Joe dutifully would take them to the post office, sometimes at two in the morning.

One of her patrons, Harold Stassen, the governor of Minnesota, proposed that his state's Whitewater State Park would have been an appropriate home for the venture.

She hired an architect named Martin Lowenfish to prepare a drawing of the proposed complex. His sketches show a family-of-man mélange of cultural stereotypes — a Dutch village with a windmill, a Chinese community with a pagoda, a Mexican village with a Mayan ziggurat, and a Turkish settlement with a minaret. Anisoara said the museum "would symbolize the peaceful pursuits and neighborliness of all nations. Each village would be peopled by first- or second-generation Americans, familiar with old-country crafts."

Sally MacDougall, a journalist with the *New York World-Telegram,* described Anisoara's project as "a miniature world in which representatives of all nations would be neighbors in a rustic community spread over 1,200 hectares (3,000 acres) containing villages, each demonstrating typical old-world crafts, arts, inns, houses, churches, clothes, cooking, modes of living, and also a central college of folk arts with workshops and classes for students."

It was the eve of World War II, and Anisoara revealed her geopolitical strategy of trying to wave the American flag while promoting an idealized version of European solidarity. She wrote: "The method of the 'melting pot' does not work ... We now know that not sameness, but diversity is what we need most. The very differences between the many groups making up the country are a source of strength, not weakness. The reason for establishing the museum now is that it would be democracy's answer to dictatorship. It would be the most powerful argument that could be used to convince the European peoples that we are for free cultural expression of all peoples. They will then know that we must also be for free political expression, as one cannot exist without the other."

NBC reporter Robert St. John covered the plan by calling Anisoara "a practical dreamer, who was a protégé of the late Queen Marie of Roumania [sic]."

According to Iosif's understanding, Anisoara positioned the

World Village as a "forerunner of the peaceful utopia of the subsequent flower power movement. It rather makes me think that it appeared out of pragmatism, and it had a well determined political purpose; it was meant to facilitate the integration of the immigrants into the American society at a time when inter-national/ethnical conflicts were putting everyone's mind ablaze."

Joe was the most intellectual of three siblings. Perhaps Anisoara recognized this and politely referred only to the physical characteristics of Joe's sisters. Anisoara described my mother: "His kid sister, Edith, was dainty, filigree, and a beautiful brunette, with big black shining eyes, and the same captivating smile like Joe. And Joe's sister, Jeanne, with auburn hair and vivacious spirit."

Joe wanted me to do well in school. At some stage I had to write a series of reports on various countries (using information mostly cribbed from the *Encyclopedia Britannica*). Joe contacted one of his artist friends who sent me hand-drawn title pages with the country names — Tibet, Japan, and India — written to resemble the distinctive calligraphy of each country. This was the trigger for my later realization that, just as almost every food can be improved with sugar, pepper, and salt, reports always benefit from graphics. Those visually improved reports, along with his support, also spurred my fascination with Asia at a time when it was just a vague, distant entity to me.

Joe had three patents (that I'm aware of).

In 1939 he received a patent for a "non-slip erasing shield to give a very sharp erasure and which will require no effort whatsoever to keep the shield from sliding."

In 1941 he came up with a "traffic control device," which featured "a visual representation of the time a light will remain on so that one can tell at a glance whether he can safely cross." It featured a descending light so a pedestrian could judge how much time remained before the green light changed to red. It's sensible, and this concept, if not the design, is used today worldwide in pedestrian lights, which count down the seconds remaining until the change of light.

And in 1944 Joe invented a "self-supporting luminaire globe," a sensible improvement to make light fixtures easier to use.

In his correspondence I also found notes from 1941 (but no patent) for a shark repellent but haven't found indication of its composition or whether he applied for a patent for this invention.

Joe was a polymath, and the world of advertising fascinated him.

I found an undated, hand-written pamphlet he wrote promoting a "completely new advertising technique" called Copy Analysis, which would evaluate advertising copy. There is no explanation what the "technique" was.

In 1953 he wrote an eight-page analysis of an Amoco tire ad, telling the company how they could improve their advertising by using his new slogan, "Sure Footed Safety," accompanied by a visual showing a cat walking on a fence.

He wrote a treatise on why "ketchup" was a better word to describe the tomato condiment than "catsup."

In 1954 he sent a letter to Julian Snyder of Erwin, Wasey & Co. advertising agency (whose creative successes included "Singin' Sam," for Barbasol shaving cream, and the coining of the term "athlete's foot," for Absorbine Jr. foot liniment), proposing an advertising idea for their client Havoline lubricating oil. Joe suggested a headline:

Slipperiness, the only true measure of a lubricating oil's worth.

No other oil in the whole world is as slippery as HAVOLINE.

And body copy:

No other oil in the whole world permits the engine parts to slide so effortlessly as HAVOLINE.

No other oil in the whole world puts less strain on your engine than HAVOLINE.

No other oil in the whole world reduces wasteful friction like

HAVOLINE.
No other oil in the whole world increases power so much like
HAVOLINE.
With a sign-off:
Get HAVOLINE
The Slippery Oil
It will keep your motor young.
And the visual:
A dignified gentleman sitting on the sidewalk after having slipped
on a banana peel.
Keeping with a motoring theme in 1953 he proposed a campaign
for Mercury automobiles:
Trouble Free Mercury
With the tagline:
You'll be Worry Free with a TROUBLE FREE MERCURY
The Car with No Regrets

While Anisoara was a skilled political animal, Joe was a well-intentioned do-gooder. In 1939 he received a reply from Goldsmith, Jackson & Brock law offices acknowledging that they would agree to represent Joe's complaint against the R.J. Reynolds Tobacco Company. I don't have Joe's initial letter, but I enjoy the notion that Joe was an early anti-cigarette campaigner. He also wrote a 1931 paper stating that "cholesterol starvation" was the cause of loss of hair, a subject of particular interest to Joe, who was bald.

I have Joe's manuscripts and notes for his papers debunking Albert Einstein. When I first thumbed through them, I thought "this man is a genius." Then I reconsidered, thinking "This man writes with the manic energy of a serial killer from the movies." Typescripts. Dozens of notes scribbled on scraps of paper. Long treatises written on yellow legal pads with complex equations and diagrams. Strong red gashes where he excised text. He was in over his head with the physics, and his correspondence file contains polite letters from leading journals and scientists telling him to stick to chemical engineering, his day job. I was reminded of a quote attributed to Nobel Prize laureate Richard Feynman: "Anyone who claims to understand quantum theory is either lying or crazy."

In his 21-page 1956 paper "The Determination of Absolute Motion," Joe boldly challenged Albert Einstein. "Pondering over the meaning of [failure to detect the ether] led Einstein to develop the Relativity Theory. ... The postulate that it is impossible to detect the absolute motion of a body through space by any physical experiment ... I will attempt to show that ... on the contrary, relative motion has no fundamental meaning, that the Relativity equations being based on the concept of relative motion are not true and that an absolute frame of reference does exist. New equations will be developed, ones that do not lead to contradictions."

I have no idea what any of this means.

He jotted down thoughts for a paper titled "Absolute Space, Absolute Time, Absolute Motion."

His notes on items such as "Calculations on Size and Collapsing Atoms" explain that: "Vol of proton = $1/25 \times 10\ 12 = 1/91125 \times 10\ 45$." His ideas are written on scraps of colored paper. Maybe this is the unheralded work of a genius, similar to a lost folio for an undiscovered Shakespeare play or sketches for Beethoven's never-achieved Tenth Symphony.

In another paper, "On the Velocity of Propagation of Gravitational Force," he again challenges Einstein: "It is therefore the purpose of this article to prove that gravitational force is propagated, not with the speed of light, but with infinite velocity."

What struck me is not that he's got his physics wrong, but the civility of the people he dealt with. The letters on file include numerous letters from journal editors who thanked him for his contribution, politely disagreed with him, and took the time to offer several pages of notes.

Even when people were rude, they were polite. In 1956 a James A. Coleman, of the department of physics at Connecticut College replied to Joe's paper: "I think that you show good general reasoning ability, but due to your meagre knowledge of elementary physics, your work has no scientific value. ...I strongly recommend that you take an evening course in general physics." In the margin, Joe wrote "What nonsense! He misses the whole point."

In another exchange, in 1959 Joe sent a short, handwritten, informal note to the Harvard Observatory in Climax, Colorado:

> "Dear Sirs, I would like very much to get some information on the sun's atmosphere ... The first layer, I believe, is the reversing layer, then comes the chromosphere, and finally the corona. I would like to know for each of these layers 1. its height, 2. its chemical composition, and 3. its temperature. Assuring you of my thanks, I am, Yours sincerely."

The director of the observatory (which was the High Altitude Observatory of the University of Colorado, with no association with Harvard University) sent him a detailed letter apologizing for the delay in responding and giving detailed answers to his questions. A kinder era in our society.

One curious aspect of Uncle Joe's life was that he and Anisoara bought an isolated farm in New York State's Adirondack Mountains. Joe didn't drive, and it took at least a day by train and bus for the couple to travel to the farm from Manhattan. I'm not sure whether they had indoor toilets. I remember Joe as a city boy and can't figure out why he would buy such a large — 115 hectares (284 acres) — rustic property. Maybe he had an idealized dream of living a modified-Thoreau existence, if only for a few weeks at a time. (I really like the idea of Joe as an unlikely woodsman.) Or maybe, and this explanation makes more sense, he bought the farm to keep Anisoara happy, since the landscape reminded her of her youth in rural Transylvania. I have some photos taken at their seven-room house; he is wearing a plaid lumberjack shirt, and she is wearing a tunic-like dress and styles her hair in a sort of Transylvanian Princess

Leia-like coif.

In 1955, after Anisoara died, Joe wanted to sell the property (asking price $15,000); he described the place to a realtor as having "soul stirring views on top of Thompson Mountain."

I vaguely recall my first visit to the Adirondack house, in the village of Stony Creek, about an hour from Lake George. I was a young child, maybe four or five. It had taken us all day to drive from New Jersey in my father's Buick. It was an old house, smelling of the forest and dead mice. There was a pond, which I was warned not to go too close to. Then a long drive back to New Jersey.

In 2015 my wife and I returned to Uncle Joe's and Anisoara's farm. I not only found the Stony Creek website (town slogan: "The road to a friendly town is never long") but also contacted the town's historian, Cindy, who was intrigued by my quest and took a day off work to show us around.

The big red house is still there but was unoccupied when we visited. Cindy said she thought the owner was coming up a few days after we were scheduled to leave, and I left a note for him under the front door explaining my interest and asking him to please contact me. I have no idea what I expected, maybe an invitation to stop by for coffee next time I'm in the neighborhood. I just wanted a connection with the old place. Never heard from the guy.

Joe had made a map of the property showing the house and pond. We looked around, in the rain, but couldn't find the pond. Then we went back the next day, and it was right there, right where it should have been if you turned the map on its side, just a few meters off the driveway. Smaller than I remembered. Still full of frogs and newts and little fish. Everything a boy needs for a summer holiday.

I posited my theory to Cindy that they bought the farm because it reminded Anisoara of Transylvania. Cindy suggested a different explanation. The area had several Americana museums and a thriving colony of craftsmen. In the post-war years, many New York intellectuals and artists bought summer places in Stony Creek, and Joe and Anisoara probably joined their friends in the summer exodus, perhaps planning to add a Romanian folk arts museum to the town's attractions.

When Joe died, my father, who was the executor of his estate, sold the farm. I remember that I bravely protested the sale, arguing that it belonged in the family, real estate would always increase in value, we could go there on vacation, and I could have it when I got older. Even though I was still a child (well, a man if you count a bar mitzvah as a genuine coming-of-age ritual), I had a bit of Joe's wanderlust and desire to live an unordinary life.

Two very different people — the brainy, idealistic, good-hearted New York Jewish nerd who lived in Greenwich Village and the complex, exotic Eastern Orthodox woman from eastern Europe with a political agenda and a sentimental heart. Did they love each other? Almost certainly. Did each make the other partner better? Absolutely. Will we ever know what their relationship was really like and what emotions they felt? Of course not. I'm the last surviving relative with even a smattering of interest in Uncle Joe. Anisoara's relatives have disappeared in the forgotten file cabinets of Romanian history. They left no children, only some documents. But through their writings we can imagine what their lives were like, and perhaps that's good enough. If Joe and Anisoara were to appear in a dream, I might see Antonino Rocca delivering a flying kick on the lumbering Mummy while eating Anisoara's *mămăligă cu brânză și smântână* in a pavilion in the World Village of Peasant Art, just as my parents cruise into the driveway, looking at their watches and happily grumbling "Joe is going to spoil that boy."

In Search of ...

SCOUNDRELS AND WANNABE LEGENDS

Almost a Knight to Remember

I Rather Liked Being Called "Sir Paul"

Adobe Stock/Michelle

The author, practicing his knight posture,
before declining the honor.

I turned down a knighthood recently. It was a tough decision — I liked the sound of "Sir Paul."

I had replied to a notice in the *International Herald Tribune* that offered "an economically available, State Sanctioned Hereditary Knighthood."

Turns out that some wannabe nobles have resurrected the Knights Templar, a prominent and powerful group of medieval Christian noblemen who protected pilgrims on the crusader routes to Jerusalem.

43

The Knights Templar were created by the Catholic church in 1127 and were wiped out by the same folks when Pope Clement V's bull *Vox in excelso* on March 22, 1312, abolished the group, despite its being vigorously championed by notables such as Dante Alighieri. Two years later, the Church ordered Knights Templar Grand Master Jacques de Molay burned at the stake.

The literature surrounding the Knights Templar weaves historical fact, fantastical tales, conspiracy theories, metaphysics, and religious geopolitics. Some writers claim that the image of what is now called the Shroud of Turin is that of Jacques de Molay's. An abundant shadow literature claims that the Knights Templar were the origin of Freemasonry. They had links to the fabled continent of Atlantis and possessed the Ark of the Covenant and the Holy Grail. You might remember them as supporting characters in Dan Brown's *Da Vinci Code*.

Several years ago, a group of mostly British visionaries recreated, in Israel, the Ancient and Noble Order of Knights Templar as a non-profit organization. For just a single $5,000 charge and dues of $500 year (less than my golf club fees), I could be honored in an investiture involving apanages and escutcheons. I'd get to wear a special ring, have use of two castles, and the opportunity to buy privately bottled Knights Templar Bordeaux.

And even better, the title comes with citizenship of a new country they're creating, code-named Savantis.

Knights Templar Chancellor Savant Graham Renshaw-Heron had asked to visit me, a recruiting mission, I thought, and I invited him to lunch at my golf club. He happily got stuck into a bottle of Côtes du Rhône and explained their plans: "Only five people know where Savantis is." He refused to tell me where it was, but from reading between the lines, I figure they're buying an island in the Caribbean. Sir Graham, enjoying his wine, explained that the thousand or so locals are enthusiastic about becoming Savantists and living under five dukes who will control the country. The nation will become a beacon of hearty, mostly British-bred, capitalistic enthusiasm, with economic benefits accruing from the planned casinos, resorts, golf courses, offshore banking, and flags-of-convenience shipping.

I asked my friend Dan about whether he too wanted to sign up — I figured we could get a two-for-one deal, maybe even a free toaster. "Those guys don't need their own country," Dan said. "They're already on their own planet."

The Knights Templar certainly have a history of geographical expansion. The medieval group had a fleet larger than that of most countries — Columbus flew the Templar's red cross on his sails. William Mann, author of *The Labyrinth of the Grail*, claims that the Knights Templar "possessed the 'secret' of being able to fix longitudinal positions long before it became common practice," and this "sacred geometry" allowed Neolithic-to Roman-era "societies who were in on the secret" to circumnavigate the world and settle corners of the world that are far removed from Europe.

So, the idea that the new Knights Templar might start their own country has a certain fuzzy logic — after all, the original Knights Templar bought the island of Cyprus.

Similarly, Sir Graham assured me that Savantis (Latin for "savior") is "just an inch away from receiving UN recognition." I could see myself as social director at the Savantis Golf Club, perhaps, or professor of creative writing at Savantis University.

One thing is sure, though: There will never be a Gay Pride Day in Savantis. Although the Knights Templar constitution preaches "there are no, nor shall there ever be, any political, religious or racial affiliations, obligations or favours of any nature," the group draws the line on the issue of homosexuality. They are very clear: "While it may be recognized that certain governments, and for their own reasons, have decriminalized acts of homosexuality, it is the avowed policy of this Noble Order to unreservedly condemn and decry all such activities."

A cynic might smirk at the group's historic disavowal of

homosexuality. The story goes back to the morning of October 13, 1307, when Jacques de Molay, the group's founder, was arrested. He spent the next seven years in prison undergoing extreme torture to force him to issue a confession that would damn the order in the eyes of the people and the Catholic Church. Although de Molay confessed under duress to denying Christ and trampling on the Holy Cross, he steadfastly denounced the accusations that the initiation ritual consisted of homosexual practices.

I don't like the idea of Savantis telling people how to run their lives. Nevertheless, I grudgingly admire the Knights Templar's libertarian spirit, encouraging the "abandoning of all wimpish thoughts whether this or that cannot or should be attempted."

The Knights Templar documentation is boisterously individualistic and would appeal to anyone who thinks there is entirely too much government in our lives. Savantis will be a place where: "further and more self-evident human rights, such as the absence of oppressive alimony laws, childish seat belt laws, alcoholic consumption laws, the punishment of success by the successful being forced to support the unsuccessful, or the energetic being obliged to support the slothful, shall also be Constitutionally and conspicuously absent, while the inherent rights of self defence, privacy, protection of property, etc. shall be immutably enshrined in The Constitution of Savantis, which shall become blended with the Constitution of this Noble Order... ."

It's their right, of course, to decide who can become a Savantis citizen and what the codes of sexual ethics are. Northern Australia, among many places, prohibits homosexuality. Ownership of more than six dildoes is illegal in Texas, while in Indiana, "covered male genitals in a discernibly turgid state" are illegal in public. And adultery will, theoretically at least, get you arrested in New York.

I ordered another bottle of wine and questioned the civil liberty issue. Sir Graham argued: "Your golf club wouldn't allow me to play in just a bathing suit. They're allowed to set their own standards of behavior. So are we."

And I liked the sound of Sir Paul. The truth is, I was tempted. I left myself a phone message ("Sir Paul, this is Steven Spielberg. I'd like to make a film of your novel.") to see how it sounded. It sounded just fine. Full disclosure: Other acquaintances have called me more colorful titles.

But I've always rejected honors. I refused to join the high school honor society and a college fraternity. With the exception of my golf club, I'm sympathetic to Groucho Marx's dictum that he wouldn't join any club that would have him as a member.

But still, "Sir Paul" has a certain ring (and a reasonable price tag). Maybe I was too hasty. I could possibly work my way up the Templar Totem Pole of Nobility. Since I'm a writer, I could eventually be known as "The Prince Formerly Known as Artist.

THE *REAL* FIRST WHITE RAJAH OF BORNEO

How Can You Become King or Queen (Your-Name-Here) the First?

Alexander Hare issued his own coins for his kingdom in Maluka, southern Borneo. Shown here is a *duit mathrif* (market doit) with an inscription in Jawi script and the date 1813.

MALUKA, KALIMANTAN, INDONESIA

I belong to a small group of people curious about the life and times of Alexander Hare. When we get together, we ponder an improbable question: How did an ambitious 19th-century slave-owner, harem-builder, and political arriviste become the First White Rajah of Borneo?

The bigger question: How does one become king or queen numero uno? More specifically, how might I become the first Supreme Leader With Wisdom Like Solomon Whose Eyes Spot Prey Like an Eagle and Whose Courage Rivals That of a Tiger of my own country?

Turns out it's a bit like becoming a star baker. Follow the

instructions, have some innate talent and creativity, hire a good PR agent, and create a made-for-TV backstory that preferably involves wondrous miracles, military victories, and a direct line of descent from a notable divinity. Add a dollop of anti-establishment vigor and a bucket of renegade cheek, and you're on your way.

⸻◆⸻

First, a quick quiz for students of Asian history. Who was the first White Rajah of Borneo? No points if you answered Sir James Brooke, the Englishman who was appointed Rajah of Sarawak in 1841 by the Sultan of Brunei for fighting pesky Dayak headhunters on the sultan's behalf. James Brooke was rewarded with the territory of Sarawak to govern as he saw fit.

The true first White Rajah of Borneo was the Englishman Alexander Hare, who had his moment in the Borneo sun some 30 years before James Brooke.

Hare left behind no monuments, no lasting social innovations, no glittering palaces, not even a flattering "swagger portrait" as was often commissioned by proud British nobles. He was not a patron of the arts nor was he keen on landscaped gardens. What he did leave were hundreds of illegitimate children and thousands of miserable slaves.

Alexander Hare (1775–1834) was an English merchant who joined a trading company in Portugal around 1800, then moved to Calcutta several years later where, according to apocryphal legend, promptly set up housekeeping with a 14-year-old dancing girl named Dishta.

He later settled in the Malaysian port of Malacca, where he met Stamford Raffles, soon to be the lieutenant governor of British Java (sorry, this gets confusing; the Malaysian city of Malacca has no relation to Hare's territory of Maluka in Borneo — which is sometimes written Moluko, Molucco, Molukko, or Maloekoe — nor to the far eastern Indonesian Maluku Islands, also known as the Moluccas). Hare had already exhibited his proclivity for young women, and Raffles's biographer, Tim Hannigan, says that in Malacca, Hare ran "a highly irregular household with barely post-pubescent Asian women of various races tumbling out of every bedroom."

With these sterling credentials for foreign service, Raffles sent Hare to Borneo in 1812 to become Political Commissioner of the government for the native states in Borneo and Resident of Banjarmasin (technically, the term referred to a diplomatic post, but in reality, the resident was responsible for ensuring the ruler adhered to his treaty agreements).

During the 1811–1816 British Interregnum, when England took temporary control over Java from the Dutch (who were busy losing battles closer to home against Napoleon), Raffles responded to a request from Sultan Sulaiman al-Mutamidullah of Banjar for help in suppressing lawlessness and piracy (similar to the reasons the Sultan of Brunei sought the assistance of James Brooke some three decades later). Raffles saw the opportunity to establish an exclusive trading relationship — timber, gold, and diamonds among the most valuable commodities — with Banjarmasin, located on the southern tip of the island of Borneo, and appointed Hare to establish the bond.

The sultan welcomed the economic benefits and military protection such a treaty with Britain would provide, and as a sign of good intent (or as a generous bribe), gave Hare a chunk of swampy, unproductive land six-times the size of Singapore.

It was hardly a salubrious base, but Hare wasn't picky. He set himself up as ruler of a personal kingdom called Maluka, issued his own coinage, and indulged in a personal business that was illegal in British-controlled Indonesia: slavery.

He also pursued his predilection: young women. Lots and lots of young women.

Shortly after Hare arrived in Banjarmasin, he immediately broke East India Company policy and Raffles's own regulations for British Residents at native courts. A resident was not allowed to accept any kind of gift from a king, including gifts of land. (Perhaps trying to distance himself from Hare, Sultan Sulaiman later complained that Hare's land was meant to be used for his private residence and was not intended to house unruly convicts who frightened the local citizens.)

And the women running around servicing Hare, well, that just wasn't the way British colonial officials were expected to behave.

⸻◆⸻

According to the few historians who bother to study him, Alexander Hare was either a talented diplomat who secured a strategic treaty with an important sultan, or an egocentric, law-breaking scoundrel who used his position to assuage his own needs.

In his reports Raffles praised Alexander Hare, saying that under his administration, Banjarmasin had been "reduced to order and regulation." Raffles effused that Hare was "a gentleman whose desire after useful knowledge and whose zealous exertions in the cause he has undertaken, are perhaps unrivaled." Parroting Raffle's praise, British diplomats reported that Hare "had been received at the Sultan's Court with the most particular respect and attention, and had been hailed throughout his Highness's [George III] dominions as the deliverer of that once powerful Kingdom."

Not so, according to Tim Hannigan, author of *Raffles and the British Invasion of Java*: "The truth was that under Hare, Banjarmasin was reduced to poverty, disorder, and unprofitability."

Historian Graham Irwin also takes a negative view, writing that Hare was "plausible, unscrupulous, and ambitious [and whose] desire was to found a kingdom of his own where he could luxuriate in oriental splendour surrounded by slaves and ladies of the harem."

But Raffles defended Hare, noting that the strategy to engage the sultan had been Hare's and there was not "any other person competent from local knowledge or respectability of character to whom the charge could have been entrusted."

So, was appointing Hare a brilliant tactic or something Raffles would privately regret?

The general consensus is that appointing Hare was one of Raffles's least successful management decisions. According to Hannigan, Hare was guilty of "unhinged despotism, flagrant disregard for British colonial law, and outright sexual excess."

Hare's blatant extravagances, oversized testosterone surge, and outrageous arrogance led to a colonial embarrassment and two jolly British colonial sound bites, known interchangeably, as the Banjarmasin Enormity and the Banjarmasin Outrage.

<hr>

Accompanied by my friend Joe Yas, I searched for Alexander Hare's kingdom, located an hour's easy drive south of Banjarmasin, a rambling city of some 700,000 in southern Kalimantan.

We visited a flat, featureless region of floodplains and muddy tidal estuaries, just a step up from a swampy morass, with rice paddies, rubber gardens, a pineapple plantation, and large windowless blockish houses designed to attract swiftlets whose saliva-constructed nests are the key ingredient in bird's-nest soup. Here and there we passed the on-road commerce that one finds throughout Indonesia — motorcycle dealers, small restaurants offering duck rice, a few shops.

Some palaces are built on dramatic promontories or at strategic confluences of rivers. But the location of Hare's palace is easy to overlook. Joe, who is a senior guide, a sterling raconteur, and a man-with-a-mission look in his eyes, stopped at the mouth of Sungai (River) Kurau, where we found a few scattered ruins from a long-forgotten fort. This location, in a protected harbor just a couple of kilometers from the sea, was a likely location for Hare's palace.

We were welcomed into local homes in the nearby village of Maluka Baulin — the term "baulin" or "ba-ulin" refers to the iron-wood trees once found in abundance in the region. The tree is native to the lowland rainforests of Sumatra and Borneo and is listed as vulnerable in the International Union for Conservation of Nature Red List due to extensive logging. Its extremely durable wood is still prized to construct Indonesia's distinctive *phinisi* sailing boats.

In the Lambung Mangkurat Museum, outside Banjarmasin, we had spoken earlier with a museum curator, Slamet, who showed us a scale model of a large wooden house of the period. Was this the type of elegant Malay-styled mansion Hare built for himself on this site — a swampy inlet with direct access to the sea, the location from where he ran his empire trading in ironwood and building sea-worthy ships to export Borneo's riches and import young women?

———◇———

Countries are being created and destroyed all the time. The United States, of course, didn't exist before 1776, and it has undergone numerous geographic changes since. Italy didn't exist before 1866, and even then, it was missing Rome, which joined in 1870. A vast swath of African and Asian countries were mere pink blotches on the straight-lined colonial maps before the post-World War II period, and the 1990's breakup of the Soviet Union and Yugoslavia created nation-building opportunities for many territories that previously were known only to geographers and stamp collectors. The UN had just 99 member states in 1960, but this number expanded quickly — South Sudan became the 193rd and most recent UN member in 2011.

New countries require leaders, whether they be presidents, kings or queens, celestial emperors, beloved leaders, grand wizards, or lord high executioners. These leaders might be muffin-like grandparent-types or trident-wielding war-mongering bloodthirsty pirates. But how difficult is it to create a new country? The world is awash in micro-nations, defined by *Encyclopedia Brittanica* as "an entity that claims to be an independent state but whose sovereignty is not recognized by the international community."

There is an international convention for being able to call a geographical entity a true country. The Montevideo Convention on the Right and Duties of States, accepted by 198 signatory states, and adopted by the League of Nations in 1933, says that any entity that meets its four criteria — population, territory, government, and the capacity to enter into negotiation with other states — can be regarded as sovereign under international law. Note that under the Convention a country does not have to be recognized by other states; it only has to have the capacity to do so.

So, why not give it a go?

Some people are already from a noble family and want to move up the royal totem pole. Such was the case with Nancy Valerie Brooke, the third daughter of Charles Vyner Brooke. Nancy was third (and last) of Sarawak's White Rajahs whom reporters dubbed "The Siren of Sarawak" and "Princess Baba." She dreamed of buying an island in the Netherlands East Indies (Indonesia) with her professional wrestler husband. She was going to name it "Babaland," where "every man would be Rajah." In his book *Sylvia, Queen of the Headhunters*, Philip Eade quoted Nancy as saying, "We're going to have a democracy but with a court and things — maybe an aristocratic democracy. I think a country without lots of uniforms and braids is no fun."

But what options exist for commoners?

A wannabe emperor might heed the advice of His Excellency President Grand Admiral Colonel Doctor Kevin Baugh, the founder and president of the Republic of Molossia. His house and garden near Reno, Nevada, form the nation's territory, population 27, which boasts a flag, stamps, currency, customs house, radio show, and post office.

Baugh's advice for people who want to start their own nation:

"First off, use your imagination. It's not necessarily all an imaginary thing, but it requires you to think outside the box when you're starting your own country. Learn about what other nations do. You know, learn a little bit of history — how countries have started and eventually stopped. And then, of course, build it from what you know. Your flag should represent you and your country — your coat of arms, all that kind of thing."

About the time that Hare was installing himself and his concubines in Maluka, in 1811 an American whaler named Jonathan Lambert declared himself sovereign and sole possessor of the island group he named the Islands of Refreshment. The idyllic name for his kingdom was not due to the islands' swimming pools and piña coladas but because the islands were transit stops for restocking supplies used by American cruisers sent to prey on British merchant ships. The islands, now named Tristan da Cunha, are part of the British overseas territory of Saint Helena, Ascension and Tristan da Cunha. They form the most remote inhabited archipelago in the world, lying roughly midway between Argentina and South Africa.

✳

For $145, you can become a citizen of the Principality of Castellania in Austria, where Prince Ralph I, formerly a burgher named Otto Hubner, has sold more than 2,000 citizenships in 25 years of independence.

✳

In November 1998, Philippines police raided a hotel in Olongapo, near Subic Bay, and arrested a Briton, an Australian and a Malaysian. They had been running an internet scam that offered passports for a fictitious nation called the Dominion of Melchizedek, named after Jerusalem's high priest who blessed Abraham after he rescued his son Lot and his family from Sodom.

The Dominion of Melchizedek's bubble burst when a man who identified himself as "His Serene Highness Gerald-Dennis Sayn-Wittgenstein-Hohenstein" tried to open bank accounts in Hong Kong with checks issued by phony Melchizedek banks. The 22-year-old unemployed Austrian, who had been living in the passenger terminal at Kai Tak airport in Hong Kong, turned out to be a baker, not a prince. During his trial, it was discovered that he had visited several Asian countries with his Melchizedek "diplomatic passport." He was convicted for bank fraud and jailed for six months.

✳

In the geographical United States, you could become a citizen of the Republic of Roadkills-R-Us, whose motto is "Tread on Me."

✳

In 2015 a Czech named Vit Jedlicka proclaimed the Free Republic of Liberland on seven square kilometers (three square miles) of land that was previous *terra nullius*, unclaimed by either Serbia or

Croatia — a quirk of an ongoing border dispute between the two former Yugoslav countries. One attractive provision in the nation's proposed constitution "significantly limits the power of politicians so they could not interfere too much in the freedoms of the Liberland nation." Applications for citizenship are accepted only by email, since Liberland does not have a post office.

Indian gurus have embraced the nation-building dream.

Maharishi Mahesh Yogi, the creator of transcendental meditation and the guru to the Beatles and Beach Boys, created the Global Country of World Peace in 2000 in the U.S. state of Iowa.

Arnoldo Chamorro, chief of staff for Paraguay's agriculture ministry, was sacked in 2023 for signing a "proclamation" with representatives of the United States of Kailasa, supporting their admission in the U.N. as "a sovereign and independent state." The micro-nation of Kailasa, which their website describes as the "revival of the ancient enlightened Hindu civilizational nation, which is being revived by displaced Hindus from around the world," is led by self-styled guru Nithyananda Paramashivam, who is a fugitive wanted in the Indian state of Karnataka on charges of rape. Representatives of the fictional polity of Kailasa have managed to participate in two UN committee meetings in Geneva and the micro-nation has entered into cultural partnerships and sister-city agreements with some 30 cities, including Newark, New Jersey; Dayton, Ohio; and Richmond, Virginia. Two members of the U.S. Congress — Norma Torres (D-California, who sits on the House Committee on Appropriations) and Troy Balderson (R-Ohio) have granted Kailasa "special congressional recognition."

Many young girls play at being princesses, but seven-year-old Emily Heaton's father decided to make her a real princess.

Jeremiah Heaton, who lives in the American state of Virginia, searched online for unclaimed land. He found Bir Tawil, an arid region on the border between Sudan and Egypt that nobody seemed to want.

In 2014 he obtained permission from Egyptian authorities to travel to the rocky patch of desert, some 20-times larger than Manhattan, where he planted a blue flag with a crown and four stars and (rather unimaginatively, for my taste) named it the Kingdom of North Sudan.

"I founded the nation in love for my daughter," he said.

Jeremiah says he's confident that the African Union will welcome him and the Kingdom of North Sudan, even though neither he nor his family have ever lived in the nation.

Princess Emily shows signs of becoming a visionary ruler; she wants to make the kingdom into an agricultural production center.

✳

Another nation-building role model is Lawrence W. Swan, an American biologist specializing in the ecology of the Himalayan region, where he searched for the jumping spiders of Everest, the springtail fly, and the ever-elusive yeti (which he concluded was a large mountain fox whose peculiar hopping gait left footprints that appeared to be those of a biped). He had the distinction of discovering two new species and having them named after him: a Himalayan frog, *Rana swani* and a flea found only in glaciers, *Machilanus swani*. More to the point of this chapter, Swan once "seceded" from both the US and Redwood City, California, protesting the order that he replace — at his own considerable expense — his "perfectly adequate and more efficient septic tank" with neighborhood sewer lines.

He anointed himself "Raja" of his own autonomous native-state, which he named the Kingdom of Cooch Nahai, a Hindi name meaning "absolute no have" or the State of Absolutely Nothing.

As the *San Francisco Chronicle* reported: "Fortunately, [Swan] made a concession to the government's right of eminent domain and continued to pay his taxes. But that did not stop him from providing Cooch Nahai with everything a small country needs. Cooch Nahai printed its own stamps — an annual philatelic issue containing the image of a forgotten element of natural history. It had a national holiday, June 21, the summer solstice; a national symbol, the extinct dodo bird; its memorial "Tomb of the Unknown Frog"; and the Great Wall of Cooch Nahai, which contained "mementos of global travels and conquests."

The antithesis to Alexander Hare's misogynist kingdom is the hard-line misandrist Other World Kingdom, a resort/micro-nation in the Czech Republic, with its own currency, passports, police force, and courts. Its goal: "To get as many male creatures under the unlimited rule of Superior Women on as much territory as possible." To become a citizen, "a woman must own at least one male slave."

Perhaps I'm insufficiently arrogant and eccentric to start my own country. But still, it's a fun exercise, one which you might like to join. So proudly sing your national anthem (mine is "Jumpin' Jack Flash"), admire your national flower (Rafflesia), salute your national flag (golf clubs rampant), offer fresh marigolds to your national protective deity (Ganesha), tip your hat to the number-one secondary deity (Dinanukht), establish a national unit of measurement (the smoot), and breed your national critter (tardigrade). Final step: Print some business cards with your royal crest and a subtle HM for His/Her Majesty.

CHINA'S EMPEROR IS TANNED, RESTED, AND READY

Homeless Hawaiian Heir to the Throne Seeks Financial Support to Restore Ming Dynasty Greatness

inf.news

Wannabe Chinese Emperor Elmer claims to be a direct descendant of the Ming Emperors. Shown is Chongzhen Emperor Zhu Youjian, the 17th and last emperor of the Ming dynasty (r. 1627-1644), as well as the last ethnic Han to rule over China before the Manchu Qing (Ching) conquest. Emperor Elmer did not allow me to take his photograph, so it is impossible to ascertain whether he bears a family likeness to Emperor Zhu Youjian.

HONOLULU, HAWAI'I

I had naively thought that China's 2,000-year-old imperial system ended when 12-year-old Aisin-Gioro "Henry" Puyi, the last emperor, was overthrown in 1912.

"Not so," declared Elmer. "I'm the last emperor."

I met the man I'll call Elmer by chance. He stood next to me in front of the visitors' board at the East-West Center in Honolulu.

"There are some Chinese visiting," he observed sotto voce, as if he was speaking in spy code.

We began to talk. Elmer was suspicious at first. He is Chinese and royal. I am Anglo and common.

Elmer is obviously an emperor of the people. Plain gray T-shirt. Dirty jeans. Flip-flops. Black hair, speckled gray, pulled into a ponytail. His briefcase was a folded piece of cardboard, from which he extracted a complicated genealogy, which links him directly and definitively, he explained, to the 17th-century Chou dynasty as well as to Zhou Enlai, Sun Yat-sen, and Chiang Kai-shek.

But what about Prince Aisin-Gioro Puyi? I asked, referring to the younger brother of Henry Puyi, the last emperor whose life was featured in Bernardo Bertolucci's film.

"Puyi was Ching dynasty. Manchurians. Invaders. My family are true Han Chinese," Emperor Elmer said.

His genealogy, printed on the back of his CV, told a contorted tale of usurped emperors and invaders, and of exiled royalty who emigrated to Hawai'i. Shaky about Chinese family trees, I asked around and found that Elmer has been a bit, er, creative, with his historical narrative. One University of Hawai'i scholar thought that the Emperor Elmer "learned his history from a fortune cookie."

But hey, call me a dreamer. What if I invited Elmer for lunch, figuring that, just in case he was who he said he was, it couldn't hurt to be pals with the Big Guy.

Lunch stuck to cultural stereotypes. Over chop suey (Elmer) and a hamburger (me), I learned Elmer wasn't too clear about his strategy for gaining the throne. He wants to visit China, for the first time, to see his people. "Can you find funding for me?" he asks. He wants to bring Western ideas to the Middle Kingdom, particularly the religion of the Jehovah's Witnesses. "Chinese are Semites," he explains obliquely. "Direct descendants of Noah."

I suggest it might be useful for American-born Elmer to learn a few phrases of Mandarin. "Uh?" the emperor-to-be grunts, as if a new idea is like a strange food he has to ingest.

He bridles at the suggestion that he might also brush up a bit on Chinese politics and customs. He gets edgy. I've overstepped his royal space.

I ask him, respectfully, I hope, what qualifications he has to lead 1.4 billion people.

Elmer waves the genealogy. He went to college for four years but left before getting a degree, muttering, "It was a fake sexual harassment case." He adds: "I'm stable, level-headed. Have good common sense. I hope it's tough for someone to take advantage of me."

He doesn't think that China is ready for a democratic movement. What about the current generation of Chinese leaders? "They're doing the best they can."

"President [George H.W.] Bush had about the right kind of China policy," he adds. But he's down on Henry Kissinger. Elmer points out that he once handed a letter to Kissinger, who was visiting Honolulu, asking for support. To Elmer's surprise, Kissinger spent all his time in Hawai'i without seeking the emperor's counsel about how Sino-American relations would improve once Elmer took over the throne. So much for Kissinger's renowned geopolitical acumen.

⚬────◆────⚬

Obviously, self-confidence is a useful quality in a wannabe emperor. While speaking with Elmer, I was reminded of Joshua Abraham Norton, a 19th-century English Jew who sold supplies to San Francisco gold rushers, then declared himself Emperor of America.

In 1859 Norton walked into the offices of the *San Francisco Evening Bulletin* and presented them with this single sentence, which they ran on the next edition's front page:

"At the preemptory request of a large majority of the citizens of these United States, I, Joshua Norton … declare and proclaim myself Emperor of these U.S., and in virtue of the authority thereby in me vested do hereby order and direct the representatives of the different States of the Union to assemble in Musical Hall of this city, on the 1st day of February next, then and there to make such alterations in the existing laws of the Union as may ameliorate the evils under which the country is laboring, and thereby cause confidence to exist, both at home and abroad, in our stability and integrity."

It was signed "Norton I. Emperor of the United States."

Like Elmer, Norton I had a common touch: He rejected luxury and attended every public function by foot or bicycle. If he noticed someone performing some kind act, he might spontaneously ennoble the individual, from which practice the expression "Queen for a Day" was coined.

In return for his noble generosity, restaurants offered the emperor free dinners, and he was given three seats at every theatrical performance (one for himself and one for each of his famously well-behaved dogs, Bummer and Lazarus). The city paid for his uniforms, Bay Area newspapers published his proclamations, and he had his own currency printed, which was accepted widely. He had a habit of levying taxes by walking into the offices of an old business friend and announcing an imperial assessment of $10 million or so, but he could quickly be talked down to a cigar and small change. When he was arrested by an overzealous policeman "to be confined for treatment of a mental disorder," virtually every newspaper published editorials denouncing the action, and Norton was released with a lengthy public apology from the chief of police.

Norton sent frequent cables to fellow rulers offering surprisingly well-informed advice. King Kamehameha of Hawai'i (then the Sandwich Islands) was so taken with the emperor's insight and understanding that toward the end of his life Kamehameha refused to recognize the US State Department, saying he would deal only with representatives of Norton's Empire.

When Norton I died in 1890, 10,000 people lined up to view his mortal remains; his funeral cortege was three kilometers (two miles) long. At 2:39 pm during his funeral, San Francisco experienced a total eclipse of the sun.

⚜

Elmer could use some heavenly miracles since his claim to the throne is in danger of disintegrating unless he gets some support.

Elmer explained that he has high-placed relatives in the Hawaiian political and social world. "But they won't help me," he said. "They're jealous. Afraid of my power. And the CIA wants to assassinate me." I agreed not to use his real name.

We met a couple of other times, but since Elmer has no phone and no fixed domicile, it was difficult to set up appointments. We lost contact.

I read about China's political travails with renewed interest. Could it happen? I can't recall a communist state turning democratic then deciding to re-establish a monarchy. But what if … Emperor Elmer. He's tanned, rested, and ready. Emperor Elmer. I like the sound.

In Search of...

DIVINITIES
AND SOCIAL
ICONS

THE SULTAN AND THE MERMAID QUEEN
A Love Story for the Ages

Paul Spencer Sochaczewski *Paul Spencer Sochaczewski*

(Left) Wuri, one of the dancers at the bedoyo ketawang sacred ceremony honoring
the relationship between Kanjeng Ratu Kidul and the Susuhunan of Surakarta,
central Java. Wuri explained, "I had a feeling Ratu Kidul was there. One time I made
a mistake in my movement, and I felt her correcting me." There are nine dancers.
If a tenth dancer is seen, she will be the Mermaid Queen, coming to honor the king.
(Right) Illustration of Kanjeng Ratu Kidul, found at the Museum Wayang Beber
Sekartaji, outside of Yogyakarta, Indonesia.

SURAKARTA (SOLO), JAVA, INDONESIA

*T*he instructions, given by a friend of Javanese nobility, were
tantalizingly vague. If you look really carefully and if the wind is
blowing right and you are of good heart and you let yourself "switch
mode" into a semi-trance, you just might see a tenth dancer. That
would be the Mermaid Queen herself.

My friend was referring to the *bedoyo ketawang*, a sacred court

69

dance held each August in honor of the ongoing love affair between the sultans of Java and Kanjeng Ratu Kidul, a mermaid-like spirit who is considered the Queen of the Southern Ocean. In this 90-minute performance, nine dancers weave an intricate and highly stylized ritual in front of the Sultan of Surakarta, Susuhunan Paku Buwono XIII. If a tenth dancer is seen, palace-watchers say the blink-of-an-eye appearance would be the Mermaid Queen herself, come to pay her respects and reaffirm her support for the monarch.

My wife and I were on our honeymoon, travelling through Java. Through my friend's intercession, we were invited to witness this private performance.

The bedoyo ketawang reflects one of Asia's most magical *histoires d'amour* — the mystical love affair between Panembahan Senopati, a late 16th-century Javanese prince, and Kanjeng Ratu Kidul, a princess who was turned into a mermaid goddess. Together, this unlikely couple began one of the world's longest-surviving regal lines: the royal families of Surakarta and Yogyakarta, in central Java, Indonesia.

In one of many versions of the myth, a beautiful princess from the Sundanese Pajajaran kingdom of West Java was cursed by her jealous stepmother and afflicted with leprosy. In despair, the unfortunate woman went to Java's raging southern coast to meditate, where a divine voice enticed her to enter the ocean and become reborn as a powerful aquatic queen.

Shortly thereafter, Senopati, a very real Javanese ruler, was having his own *crise de coeur,* and he too headed south for prayer and contemplation. While sitting on a rock on the precipitous sea cliffs south of Yogyakarta, Senopati was seduced into the ocean by the spirit who became known as Kanjeng Ratu Kidul, the Queen of the Southern Ocean. During their three-day bacchanal in her submerged palace, he taught her the secrets of terrestrial love and she instructed him in the intricacies of good governance.

As proof of her devotion, Kanjeng Ratu Kidul promised to be the consort for all of Senopati's descendants, a tradition that is still very much recognized by the kings and sultans of Yogyakarta and Surakarta (Solo) in central Java.

In this chapter I refer to a figure known as Kanjeng Ratu Kidul. As a shape-shifting spirit, she is often conflated with a similar personage, Nyai Roro Kidul. Some scholars — and many local people — say they are the same spirit while others argue that Nyai Roro Kidul (in various spellings) is Kanjeng Ratu Kidul's prime minister, senior general, or chief of staff. For simplicity, if not constant accuracy, in this chapter I refer to her as Kanjeng Ratu Kidul, the Queen of the Southern Ocean, and, to the dismay of some, the Mermaid Queen.

Regardless of her name, the cult of Java's Queen of the Southern Sea may have originated from a much older prehistoric, Animistic, pre-Hindu-Buddhist belief — the certainty that a stern nature spirit lives in the treacherous Indian Ocean and, when she is disrespected, causes storms, tsunamis, and deaths. Most religions include powerful gods and goddesses who control the fickle power of nature, and local people well knew the dangers of being swept away by the Southern Ocean's riptide or experiencing the loss of their flimsy fishing boats in a storm. They attributed such inhospitable acts to a sea-based deity who had to be respected and appeased. In time, this watery nature spirit became anthropomorphized, mythologized, and integrated into existing beliefs and historical legends. Psychologists might argue that her existence is based on a form of deep-rooted thalassophobia, the fear of the ocean and the terrifying creatures that live in that realm.

The late Sri Sultan Hamengku Buwono IX of Yogyakarta (1912-1988) was head of arguably the most prestigious and powerful modern Javanese royal family. He was a key figure in modern Indonesia's history — he played a vital diplomatic role during the Japanese occupation in World War II and helped lead the fight for independence from the Dutch. In 1984 I was granted an audience with the sultan to discuss his relationship with Kanjeng Ratu Kidul.

In his souvenir-filled Jakarta office, he offered me sweet tea. I had one question I wanted to ask him. I tried, probably clumsily, to phrase it in a refined Javanese manner. How was it that a man as pragmatic and cosmopolitan as the sultan — he spoke several forms of Javanese as well as Bahasa Indonesia, English, and Dutch, and had been vice president of Indonesia and then held various ministerial posts — could pay homage every year to a mermaid queen?

Instead of answering directly, Sri Sultan Hamengku Buwono IX told a story. "One night during the Dutch occupation of Yogyakarta, I, and others who were living in the *kraton* [palace], heard soldiers moving noisily about, as if wearing armor. It is said they were the soldiers of Ratu Kidul protecting the palace." I pressed him for details. "As I said, there was no one in the kraton except our family and staff," he repeated. "But we all heard the soldiers' drums."

He told me about several other of Kanjeng Ratu Kidul's timely interventions that changed the course of Indonesia's history. I kept my thoughts to myself; the sultan continued, perhaps sensing my unspoken skepticism. The sultan didn't quote Shakespeare, but he might as well have. He gave me the Javanese equivalent of "there are more things in heaven and earth, Horatio/Than are dreamt of in your philosophy." He concluded: "When I was four years old, I was already living with a Dutch family, so my brain is in some ways a Western brain. But many things happen which can't be explained in a logical way."

I must have looked bewildered.

The sultan then told me not to get too caught up in a Cartesian view of the world. "You're asking a Western question, expecting a Western answer," he admonished. "You either accept it or you don't."

There is magic in the air throughout Java. Accept it or not. One man's myth-enrobed fantasy is another man's hard-nosed reality. In the rainbow-hued world of shifting Javanese cosmology, reality can be as ethereal as a wisp, like a miracle, like love. It resists dissection and flies away from analysis. Believe it or not.

Deeply held beliefs are not necessarily religious, but they often involve ritual. Sultan Hamengku Buwono IX was a cosmopolitan, well-educated man of the world. Every June 21, he trekked 20 kilometers (12 miles) to the dangerous surf on the slate-gray southern coast of Java. There he offered a full set of women's clothing and his own nail and hair clippings to pay homage. Some people might suggest this is inconsistent with his Western-influenced education. I found it admirable that he was comfortable embracing with elegance two different cultures.

Years later I put a similar who/why/what question to Trias Indra Setiawan, director of the Museum Wayang Beber Skarjati, near Yogyakarta. "Kanjeng Ratu Kidul appeared to me as a spirit when I was a young boy," he told me. "I called for my mother, but she didn't see the queen." I asked whether he could explain who or what she is. He replied: "You can't anthropomorphize her. In fact, she has no gender. She appears human, but she's not human. She is energy. Natural energy."

Visitors to Java might like to spend a night at the Samudra Beach Hotel at Pelabuhan Ratu (literally "Queen's Harbor") on the south coast of Java, scene of a dramatic appearance of the Mermaid Queen.

The story, as told to me by KRT Hardjonagoro, the regent of the susuhunan's palace in Solo:

"In 1966 Sri Sultan Hamengku Buwono IX attended the opening of the Samudra Beach Hotel, on Java's southern coast, which, of course, is Ratu Kidul's home territory," Hardjonagoro told me one evening as we nibbled some of the fried chicken for which Central Java is famous.

"In the morning, a few hours before the event, a local *lurah* [village headman] asked for an audience with the sultan. The old man told the sultan that he had had a dream the previous night in which a lady said she wanted her offerings. She was dressed in green.

"The sultan, of course, knew that the old man had seen Ratu Kidul. His Highness thanked the humbled old man but explained that he would not make an offering since he was attending the hotel opening in his civilian capacity as minister of defense, and he wanted to separate the affairs of the state from the mystical duties of the palace." We ordered more chicken, and Hardjonagoro continued. "I was outside, near the pool, when the sultan said goodbye to the well-meaning old man. Shortly after, I heard the sound of a locomotive. The noise increased until it sounded like many locomotives were coming toward the beach-front terrace where we were enjoying the hotel's hospitality. Then, suddenly, a ten-meter-high tidal wave erupted from the sea, which had been calm. It washed away the hotel's buffet table and soaked all the visitors. Some palm trees were knocked down. Someone ran to tell the sultan what had happened, and realizing what had occurred, the sultan put on his ceremonial clothes, said his prayers to Ratu Kidul, and made the appropriate offerings. The sea was calm once again."

I was incredulous. Hardjonagoro showed me the photos. I said, "Come on" or something equally un-Javanese. Instead of arguing, he simply told me to go to the hotel and ask for room 308. Sometime later, I did. This, it turns out, is the room in which Sultan Hamengku Buwono IX made peace with the easily irritated Mermaid Queen. It is kept locked and reserved only for her; however, hotel staff will allow people access so they can make offerings to the Queen of the Southern Ocean.

⸻ ◆ ⸻

The bedoyo ketawang was originally performed as a six-hour marathon, all the better to ease the dancers and audience into a trance-like state. Today, the occasional ringing of guests' cell phones reminds us that we live in a less-patient world, and the dance has been shortened to 90 minutes. Nevertheless, the atmosphere is reminiscent of a picaresque, slightly down-at-the-heels 19th-century operetta. But it is also otherworldly, with spirits in the air, as the sultan's gamelan orchestra pings and gongs a deliberate beat that accompanies a high-pitched singer. According to Nancy K. Florida of the University of Michigan, the verses first recount Senopati's setting forth to battle (or to a romantic encounter), then evoke the depth of Kanjeng Ratu Kidul's passion for Senopati and his royal successors, and end with her praise of the metaphysical potency of her royal lovers.

In the wrong frame of mind, the bedoyo ketawang can be tedious, but when I remembered my friend's advice to "switch mode," it became totally entrancing. Just as western baroque music has been shown to induce relaxation by reducing a person's heart rate and decreasing blood pressure, I have the impression that the bedoyo ketawang music, played on sacred gongs and xylophones used only on this occasion, alters our consciousness. Let's call it a Ratu Kidul-enhanced altered state.

The roadblock to transcendental experience was our location. We were seated near the front of what might be called the "commoner's section." We had poor sightlines and had to crane our necks to see past two-meter-tall statues of Greek goddesses and semi-clothed angels, huge Chinese vases, potted ferns, wrought-iron rococo balustrades, and a handful of photographers.

Nevertheless, we saw nine young women wearing sacred dark blue and white batik sarongs, colors which symbolize earth and ocean, darkness and light. They wore hair extensions pulled back in chignons entwined with golden filigree and jasmine garlands. They had been rehearsing for weeks and were forbidden to dance if they were menstruating.

⚬————◆————⚬

During the reception that followed the dance, a man named Ki Radu Kusumodiningrat approached me and asked if I wanted to "speak with Kanjeng Ratu Kidul." I wasn't too sure what he meant but said yes anyway.

Ki Radu Kusumodiningrat, a relative of the susuhunan, is a traditional healer. His colleague, Raden Ayu Retno Handayati, who was going to channel the Mermaid Queen for me, was also a distant relative; she works as an acupuncturist and massage therapist. We stopped at a market to buy fruit, candles, and incense, and went back to our hotel for the séance. The doorman busted us for the pungent-smelling durian, and out of respect for the no-smoking signs in the room, we cancelled the incense, but the medium, Raden Ayu Retno Handayati, wasn't perturbed. She put on a head scarf and intoned an Arabic blessing. Her voice shifted to the timbre of that of a young woman. She asked our names, and we suspended our disbelief and imagined we were speaking with the Mermaid Queen herself.

We asked her about her love affair with Senopati and got romantic platitudes, sort of Javanese Hallmark card sentiments.

"Were you present just now at the bedoyo ketawang?" I asked.

Raden Ayu Retno Handayati, perhaps channeling Kanjeng Ratu Kidul, smiled and answered enigmatically: "I'm always present for the sultan."

We saw she was getting tired, but just before the séance ended, Kanjeng Ratu Kidul offered me personal support and invited me on a date, Javanese Mermaid-Queen-style. "Just go to Parangkusumo [a well-known beach on the southern coast of Java], call your name, stamp your foot three times, and I will be there for you."

Raden Ayu Retno Handayati clearly went into a trance. Did she really channel the spirit of the Mermaid Queen? And what kind of reception would I get if I actually went to the beach and sought out Kanjeng Ratu Kidul? Stories are rife about men who wear green (Kanjeng Ratu Kidul's favorite color) while swimming in the Southern Ocean and are never seen again. Some logical people say such disappearances are simply victims of the treacherous riptides. However, other people know better and insist that these unfortunate men were abducted to serve the queen in her watery castle.

⸻ ◆ ⸻

I am intrigued by the possibility that Kanjeng Ratu Kidul was present at the dance and put the question to one of the bedoyo ketawang dancers. Twenty-three-year-old Wuri, a soft-spoken English teacher at a local elementary school in Solo, didn't find the question strange. "Yes, I had a feeling Ratu Kidul was there. One time I made a mistake in my movement, and I felt her correcting me."

Another dancer, 21-year-old Putri, acknowledged that toward the end of the performance she felt a current of air, as if Kanjeng Ratu Kidul was "going to the sultan."

The morning after the bedoyo ketawang, we ran into one of the susuhunan's close relatives, who was staying at the same hotel as us. Over croissants we asked the elegantly dressed woman about the previous day's performance and whether she thought that Kanjeng Ratu Kidul had appeared.

"Absolutely," she said. Her eyes started to get misty and a dreamy look, wonderful to see in a woman of a certain age, came over her face. "There was a rush of cool air. That was the queen, going to the king."

Again, I tried to ask a Cartesian question in a polite way. What did she make of all this?

In a wistful voice, perhaps more suited to a lovestruck schoolgirl, she answered, "It's a love affair for the ages."

⎯⎯◆⎯⎯

The love affair might face a breaking point.

In 2015 Sultan Hamengkubuwono X of Yogyakarta, who has no sons, named the eldest of his five daughters crown princess and declared that she would succeed him. He subsequently issued a *sabda raja* (sultan's proclamation) elevating her title to GKR Mangkubumi Hamemayu Hayuning Bawono Langgeng, which loosely means Guardian of the Eternal Beauty, Happiness and Prosperity of the World. In its simpler form, Gusti Kanjeng Ratu Mangkubumi, the title means The One Who Holds the Earth. Both names are historically given to the sultan's heir. None of the sultan's 11 brothers and half-brothers attended the proclamation ceremony.

The sultan also made the title of the monarch gender-neutral by eliminating the Arabic honorific *Khalifah*, meaning God's Steward, an Islamic title that can only bestowed upon men.

These dramatic declarations caused an uproar not only in the kraton but among the 3.8 million people of the Special Region of Yogyakarta.

Many of the people I spoke with, both within the kraton and among the general populace, feel that the title of sultan (and the accompanying appointed position as governor of Yogyakarta) must be held by a man.

The sultan's close male relatives went on a pilgrimage to the royal cemetery in Imogiri in an effort, according to one of the sultan's half-brothers, "to invoke the family's god and ancestors to change the sultan's mind."

A male cousin of the sultan, Kanjeng Raden Tumenggung Jatiningrat, added: "A female sultan is an impossibility. One symbol of this palace is a rooster — so if we have a queen, should we change it to a hen? When the sultan has left this world, we in the family have an agreement with the people that we will drive his wife and his daughters out of the palace. They will be evicted, as they will no longer be members of our family."

Aburrada Fourak, a senior imam of the prominent Gedhe Kauman Mosque, argues that "if the next ruler of the palace was a woman, she could not lead Friday prayers, a responsibility that the sultan has fulfilled throughout his family's reign."

One figure who is close to the royal families of Yogyakarta and Surakarta, was adamant, saying, "This will mark the end of both the dynasties in both Solo and Yogyakarta." The man, who has an important position in organizing ceremonial occasions, asked that he not be named. "Both current sultans have disrespected Ratu Kidul by not performing the required ceremonies or have taken her name in vain."

The sultan replied, "I don't' mind getting scolded or questioned by my brothers. I would only be afraid of getting scolded by God." He added that his decision was based on God's divine revelation, sent through his ancestors, that his successor must have a strong relationship with nature, be someone others would listen to, and must understand his or her true identity and origin.

Some younger people in Yogyakarta agree with a modernization of the sultanate and approve of the sultan's choice. "This is the up-to-date future of Yogyakarta. A queen will bring new prosperity," Dewi, an economics student at Yogyakarta's Gajah Mada University told me.

But no one, it seems, has asked the sultan's consort, Kanjeng Ratu Kidul.

Historically, the world over, all sultans, kings, rajahs, emperors, grand dukes, tsars, and emirs enhance their power through a connection with a spiritual entity. After all, what better way for a wannabe royal to stake a lineage than to claim status as the Daughter of the God of Thunder or Son of the God of Wealth. Like all great kings, the sultans of central Java benefit from a spiritual connection with the Mermaid Queen. Sacred geometry enhances that coexistence. It is said that a secret underwater/underground tunnel, used exclusively by the Mermaid Queen and the sultan of Yogyakarta, follows a straight line between Kanjeng Ratu Kidul's nautical palace in the Southern Ocean off Parangkusumo Beach, the sultan's kraton in Yogyakarta city, and the summit of the often-erupting sacred Mount Merapi to the north. Some suggest this axis is the navel of the world.

This spiritual partnership has existed for centuries. It has never been tested (or imagined) that the sultan would be a sultana. A woman.

So, the big, unanswered question is how will these two strong women relate? On the one side you have Gusti Kanjeng Ratu Mangkubumi, educated in the United States, Singapore, and Australia; a leading figure in Yogyakarta's commercial world; and immersed in kraton culture and politics. On the other side you have Kanjeng Ratu Kidul, a powerful, no-nonsense female figure who gives the sultan power and legitimacy. Will these two figures work it out like sisters and help each other? Or will Kanjeng Ratu Kidul abandon her loyalty to the throne, leaving the sultanate in limbo? Watch this space.

◦ ⸻◦⸻ ◦

Over the years I continued to seek Ratu Kidul.

In 1973, when I was at the beginning of a steep learning curve about Javan culture, a friend wanted to introduce me to a remarkable man who lived on a back street within the grounds of the kraton of Surakarta. It was almost midnight, and I said, "surely, he's sleeping; we can't disturb him." My friend, a relative of an earlier susuhunan, confidently answered, "Pak Hardjanta doesn't sleep." We took a pedaled *becak* to his simple home (a late-night ride in a trishaw, smoking a kretek clove cigarette while slowly exploring the history-enrobed perimeter of the kraton is, for me, a highlight of any trip I make to Central Java). And W. Hardjanta Pradjapangarsa was awake and chain-smoking, as if he was expecting us. I asked the usual boring fact-searching questions and Pak Hardjanta explained he had attended a Dutch Catholic school and, in his words "became a one hundred percent materialist, rejecting all that was illogical." But he became disillusioned by the "weakness of character and knowledge" of his Indonesian revolutionary idols and began a journey of isolated meditation and study, resulting in his own version of a Road to Damascus — a conversion from a devout logical Cartesian to a sage whose worldview happily embraced spirits, abstract events outside objective experience, and cosmic mysteries that cannot be dissected by formal science. His version of the spiritual world was based on the teachings of the "prophets and avatars of Indonesia." Imbued with what his followers described as *wahyu*, a "divine radiance," he taught metaphysics, Javan style, to an international group of truth-seekers. This opinionated, hunchbacked, always-squatting, elfin-man, who let his cigarette ashes drop on a fire-hazard pile of papers and books, happily explained that he was a seer who could communicate with the Mermaid Queen. He practiced a severe form of kundalini yoga, and while exposing his frail body to the mid-day sun, he learned when, to the day, the Mermaid Queen would have a fit of fury and cause Gunung Merapi volcano to erupt. I thought: Who is this voluble man with such a curious gift? What is the power of kundalini? How does one release the yogic dragon? And who is this Mermaid Queen, and why is she so angry?

✳

In 2010, I was granted an interview with Mas Penewu Surakso Hargo, better known as Mbah Maridjan, the *juru kunci* ("keeper of the key") of Mount Merapi. In his simple living room on the slopes of Mount Merapi, we spoke about his responsibilities in mediating between the sacred spirits of the natural world and the profane world of people living in modern society. He described his role as liaison between the sultan of Yogyakarta and Kanjeng Ratu Kidul, whose domain, some say, is not limited to the ocean but includes influence over Mount Merapi, one of the most active volcanoes in Indonesia. This volcano erupts, Mbah Maridjan said, when Kanjeng Ratu Kidul gets fed up with the incessant greed, arrogance, noise, pollution, and lack of spiritual respect shown by the populace.

✳

I slowly descended a series of shaky wooden ladders and gingerly followed a narrow, slippery, and vertiginous path down steep cliffs to reach Goa Langse, where an important Ratu Kidul shrine sits in a mysterious cave near the pounding surf. Some people say this is where Panambahan Senopati first met Kanjeng Ratu Kidul.

✳

I spoke with dozens of people, ranging from academics to motorcycle taxi drivers, about their experiences and whether they believed in the Mermaid Queen. Although there were not quite as many personal encounters as I found when investigating the female vampire ghosts of Pontianak, in Indonesian Borneo, they were frequent enough and of sufficient detail (elegant Javanese green sarong, long hair, aroma of rose, beautiful) to alleviate any questions about whether the Mermaid Queen retains power over the populace. And for people who hadn't had a one-on-one encounter? The consensus about whether she exists was "probably, maybe, who knows, but I think so ..."

As instructed by Raden Ayu Retno Handayati, the medium who had channeled Ratu Kidul after the bedoyo ketawang in Solo, I went to Parangkusumo Beach one evening. The night was overcast and windy, with breakers starting a hundred meters from the shoreline — broken, smudgy, fast-breaking swells, the John Cage of wave action. I stomped my foot three times. I tried to sit silently and think of her, but I'm a lousy meditator even at the best of times. The rain came. I didn't expect a golden vison of a beautiful Javanese nymph to appear, and she didn't. I retreated to the sanctuary of my car for the drive back to Yogya.

Years later, in summer 2023, I got a much better opportunity to get close to Kanjeng Ratu Kidul.

My friend Risang Yuwono, a leading photographer and promoter of a Javanese village dance troupe, arranged an interview with KRT Budi Adipuro (KRT is an abbreviation of Kangjeng Raden Tumenggung, a noble title bestowed by a sultan, roughly similar to a knighthood). KRT Budi, a large man with an engaging smile, welcomed us into his home in a village outside Yogya. He proudly showed us the devices he makes (and sells to dealers in Europe and America) that negate the effects of waves emitted by computers, cell phones, power lines, and wi-fi routers. But that's his second job. His main occupation is *juru kunci*, "key keeper" or intermediary between Ratu Kidul and the Susuhunan of Surakarta. In that position, he's the man responsible for the susuhunan's ceremonial engagements with Ratu Kidul.

I explained my decades-long interest in Kanjeng Ratu Kidul. Risang asked if we could hold a ceremony and give her offerings. KRT Budi got out his pendulum to check my spiritual health and found that four of my seven chakras (crown, heart, throat, kundalini) were open. He no doubt was also sizing me up to see if I was worthy of such an honor. We talked about Javanese philosophy, which is ever interesting and more complex each time I attempt to delve into that world. "Meet me tomorrow night after evening prayers at Parangkusumo." He gave Risang a shopping list of the offerings that would be required. And pointing at me, said, "don't wear green."

We met KRT Budi the following evening at a tea stall on the black sand beach. His first words of greeting were both ominous and promising. "I was meditating and Ratu Kidul came to me," he said. "She said she was expecting you."

I sensed he was referring to *ragasukma*, a Javanese form of astral projection practiced by spiritually developed psychics. I asked for an explanation.

"The queen says she knows you from before. You were a sea warrior. She was a mermaid when you met. 'Please,' the queen says. 'You are welcome.'"

I strip down to my (blue) swimming trunks. KRT Budi, Risang, and Risang's wife, Aurea, help me dress in traditional formal Javanese gear — a traditional Javanese outfit called *baju surjan* consisting of a brimless rounded cap (*blangkon*), a dark blue collarless woven jacket (*beskap*), and a long piece of brown and white cotton wraparound batik (*jarik*) in a parang pattern, indicating strength and strong will, which I later had sewn into a sarong. The lady who owned the tea stall watched; I couldn't tell if she was amused or impressed.

We gathered our offerings. I carried the most honored gift — a slightly rounded basket filled with white jasmine and white rose petals. KRT Budi carried a basket containing a roast chicken, bananas, and coconut that had been prepared by Aurea. Aurea had a cone of *nasi kuning* (yellow rice) that she had cooked.

"Think of something you want to ask her. And remember, the sea is dangerous. When a wave comes stand to the side, otherwise you'll be knocked down and you might be carried away."

We walked to the shore and sat on the sand. KRT Budi was aware that I don't sit comfortably in the lotus position, so he carried a rattan stool for me. "No plastic!" he said, referring to Ratu Kidul's ecological sensibility. KRT Budi drew a large circle in the sand, not unlike the witches' circle featured in countless horror movies. By now a small group of onlookers had approached, not intrusive, but politely curious — a combination of guys who just hung around the tea stalls and pilgrims of various degrees of commitment. KRT Budi gave his prayers, some spoken, some chanted, some silent. We stuck incense sticks in the sand. He slapped the sand three times and motioned us to head into the sea.

"Wait for my signal. Wait for a big wave."

Standing perpendicular to the waves we waited. I lost count, maybe ten small waves had broken around our waists. "Next wave," KRT Budi said.

The powerful wave crashed into us, around chest height. I grabbed Aurea, who was in danger of falling. As the wave began to recede, we felt the strong undertow and tried to remain upright. "Now," Budi said, and we released our offerings to be carried out to sea.

And did a miracle occur? You be the judge. It was the night of a blood supermoon, when tides are at their highest and the forces of the ocean are most active. The evening had been cloudy. When we released the baskets, some of the clouds parted and the moon shone like a searchlight over the turbulent sea.

We retreated to the beach, lit some more incense, said some more prayers, and started back to the tea stall for a cold-water bath and to change into dry clothes. A man who had been watching the event shyly approached me, holding one of the flowers I had offered to Ratu Kidul that had drifted back to the beach. "Do you mind if I keep this?" he asked.

"Of course. With the queen's blessings."

POWER BEYOND JAVA

Room 327 of the Hotel Bali Beach dedicated to Kanjeng Ratu Kidul and President Sukarno. This was the only room that was not devasted by a fire in 1992 that destroyed virtually the entire 300-room building.

"Let me show you Ratu Kidul's influence in Bali."

My old friend Anak Agung Gede Rai told me a tale involving Kanjeng Ratu Kidul, a proud Mermaid Queen-admiring national hero, an imposing architectural symbol of Indonesia's aspirations, and a hotel room that, seemingly miraculously, had been spared from a catastrophic fire that destroyed the 10-story building.

***

Rai took me to the landmark Grand Inna Bali Beach, originally named the Hotel Bali Beach, located in Sanur, a district known for magic and supernatural encounters.

The hotel was built in 1963 with funds provided by Japan as compensation for World War II crimes against the country, along with similarly grand (and similarly designed) hotels in Jakarta (Hotel Indonesia), Yogyakarta (Ambarrukmo Palace Hotel), and Pelabuhan Ratu (Samudra Beach Hotel), site of the Ratu Kidul event mentioned earlier.

I knew the hotel well, for this was where I first met Rai. He was marketing and communications director (and later general manager) of the hotel, and my ad agency in Jakarta handled the hotel's advertising. It was the most imposing building ever built on Bali and will remain so. Angry traditionalists said it was too tall and not sufficiently Balinese in spirit; subsequent legislation in 1971 restricted the height of new buildings to "shorter than the tallest coconut trees." In practice this means a height of three or four stories, depending on the health of your plantation and the height of your ceilings.

So, how does this relate to Kanjeng Ratu Kidul?

To understand the involvement of the Mermaid Queen in Bali, one has to understand the personality and cultural background of Sukarno, Indonesia's first president. He was a freedom fighter, a proponent of anti-imperialism, and a champion of the global Non-Aligned Movement.

But Indonesian leaders cannot be understood simply by their political actions. The supremely charismatic Sukarno was of mixed Javanese and Balinese descent. His belief system was rooted in the cultures of the two regions and united through a complex Hindu pedigree. He also saw himself as a form of Ratu Adil, a "just king," so promoting a relationship with Kanjeng Ratu Kidul no doubt appealed to his political-personal image of royal importance.

Sukarno took a keen interest in the construction of the large new hotels, which he felt were required to attract foreign tourists to the at-that-time impoverished country. He personally wanted to identify the location of the Bali hotel, and, he said that while flying in a helicopter over the island, Kanjeng Ratu Kidul showed him the spot in Sanur where she wanted the Hotel Bali Beach to be constructed.

⌖

In the steamy mid-day of Wednesday, January 20, 1993, some 30 years after its construction, the 300-room Hotel Bali Beach burst into flames with such ferocity that black smoke darkened the sky over Sanur. Huge tongues of flames leapt from the windows of the 10-story building. Almost miraculously, none of the 400 guests and 1,000 staff members were injured.

It was two days before the building had cooled sufficiently for officials to enter and assess the damage. They saw that steel railings on the balconies had melted. Guest passports in safe deposit boxes had burned. Every room had been destroyed.

Except for room 327.

Room 327, next to the elevator and staircase, had some smoke damage but otherwise was intact. On the side table, bottles of Aqua drinking water (another client of mine) were undamaged. The bed linen was intact and still pristine. Complementary bathrobes hung undisturbed in the closet, the pictures on the wall hung sedately.

Gina Meridiani, the hotel's duty manager who accompanied us to the room, said it is a "miracle" this room was undamaged. The only explanation, she suggested, is that this room had divine protection.

After the fire subsided, physical repair began. But in Bali, when there is a calamity, there is also a need for a spiritual cleansing, so some 10 days after the conflagration, Rai asked a senior Balinese priest to perform a ritual in the unscathed room. The priest, clad in white, went into a trance and saw a man. "Sorry, who are you?" the priest asked. "I'm Sukarno," the spirit answered, and offered three messages related to the fire:

The first comment was "don't worry about the fire, the hotel will be rebuilt soon." And it was. The reconstruction took less than eight months.

Second, the spirit of Sukarno said, "The fire is the fire of revolution. There will be a big change in the country soon." And this is where fans of Nostradamus-like prophecies can enjoy themselves. Was Sukarno's 1993 spirit referring to the 1998 overthrow of the military regime of his successor Suharto, which led to a flowering of Indonesian democracy? Or are such prophecies not worth burning even a single brain cell to figure out?

Third, the Sukarno spirit instructed that room 327 should be kept as a permanent shrine to the Mermaid Queen, whom the Balinese call Ida Ratu Kidul. She easily fits into the Balinese world-view and conflates comfortably with the similar Balinese Queen of the Sea, known as Batara Segara (also called Ida Bhatara Kasuhun Kidul). According to Anak Agung Gede Rai, she is sometimes considered a version of Durga or Kali, the fierce avatars of Shiva's consort Parvati. In Bali she is usually portrayed as the dangerous old witch Rangda, which many tourists will have seen in the Barong dance. Like Durga and Kali, Rangda is the evil that balances the good — a necessary and vital role. But black and white shifts easily into grey — threatening spirits like Rangda (and Kanjeng Ratu Kidul) are rarely entirely bad, and the benevolent gods are rarely entirely good. Sort of like people.

⸺◆⸺

I took off my shoes and was allowed into the room. The wallpaper was brown from smoke, the wooden cupboards and cabinets were undamaged, the twin beds were intact, the decades-old pale-green carpet and the Bakelite telephone were unscathed. I parted the flimsy curtains and saw a pleasant view of the hotel garden and the sea.

But the offerings of pilgrims had made the space into a cluttered and eclectic shrine. Photos of Sukarno looking confident and smiling his seductive grin. An Indonesian flag. Many pairs of ladies' shoes. Images of Ganesha. An antique kris. Incense and plastic flowers. And, sitting on a shrine, a copy of a famous painting of Kanjeng Ratu Kidul.

After some 10 minutes of respectful silence, Gina asked us to leave, explaining: "A couple is getting married in the hotel tomorrow, and they've come to ask for Ratu Kidul's blessing."

Ganesha and Santa Claus
Two World-Famous Personalities Separated at Birth?

Adobe Stock/CravenA   *Adobe Stock/Evhen Pylypchuk*

Ganesha and Santa Claus. The similarities are too great to ignore.

MUMBAI AND NORTH POLE

Some people (well, me, primarily) have compared the generous Hindu elephant-headed god Ganesha to the similarly kind-hearted Santa Claus. They are remarkably similar, and anthropological genealogists (a couple of my friends who took Anthro 101 at university) consider the two personalities to be at least first cousins, and possibly twin brothers, separated at birth. We await DNA analysis.

Here's the 16-point evidence:

1. Morphology

   Both Ganesha and Santa Claus are rotund.

   Two of Ganesha's 108 names are Lambodara (Pot Belly) and Mahodara (Great Belly). His big stomach can be explained in

89

two ways. First, he has swallowed all the troubles of the world to protect mankind from suffering. Second, his cosmic beer belly is necessarily large to contain the wisdom of all universes — past, present, and future.

Santa Claus's robust figure, which has been described as "a little round belly that shook when he laugh'd, like a bowl full of jelly," is due to the perils of Western civilization. He lives a couch-potato existence during most of the year. He sits comfortably in his North Pole hideaway, supervising, by remote closed-circuit TV, thousands of undocumented elves who make up his toy-making workforce. In his leisure time it is thought he does not exercise but instead relaxes in front of the fire, thinking about how to make children happy while enjoying his wife's home-baked cookies.

2. **They Were Created About the Same Time**
   The first records of Ganesha date to the 4th to 5th centuries CE.

Santa Claus's precursor was Saint Nicholas, a 4th-century CE Greek Christian bishop who lived in what today is Turkey. A devoutly pious Christian, Saint Nicholas is usually portrayed as a full-bearded cleric in red ceremonial robes and was noted for offering generous gifts to the poor.

3. **Making a List of Who's Been Naughty and Nice**
   Ganesha keeps a record of who's been nice (in his worldview that means upholding Hindu dharma). He doesn't remove obstacles simply because someone asks; he insists that the devotee make an appropriate offering and be of good heart.

Santa Claus not only has a list, but he checks it twice.

4. Sweet Tooth, Lactose-Tolerant

Both Ganesha and Santa Claus enjoy sugary delicacies and a glass of milk.

Ganesha's favorite treats are sweet dumplings called *modak* (central India) or *laddu* (north India). They are shaped like money parcels, related to Ganesha's ability to help a believer become wealthy.

And Ganesha has a well-documented love of milk, evidenced by a "milk miracle" that occurred in September 1995 when a devotee in New Delhi saw a Ganesha statue "drink" a spoonful of milk that was offered. This event was soon followed by dozens of similar events, creating a nationwide sensation that quickly went global.

Indian soldiers on the western border with Punjab stopped their maneuvers to worship Ganesha. The Bombay and Delhi stock exchanges closed while traders offered milk to Ganesha. A rumor spread that an elephant-headed boy, a possible reincarnation of Ganesha, had been born that morning in a Punjab town. The right-wing Hindu political parties pounced on this sensation (some cynics say they instigated it) declaring the milk-drinking was a "prophecy" that they would win the general election the following year. (The 1996 election produced a hung parliament with no single party having a clear majority.) The phenomenon, which had rapidly spread globally, stopped as quickly as it had started. Indian scientists proved that the "miracle" was caused by a combination of surface tension and capillary effect.

Santa Claus is known to appreciate homemade cookies and a glass of cold milk that is waiting for him when he makes a home visit. (Note: One Christmas I awoke to find a note from Santa: "Thanks for the milk, but next year perhaps you might leave a beer.")

5. **Flashy Outfits and Unique Style Sense**
    Ganesha is pictured with powerful symbols of his importance.
    He often sits on a throne in what is called the "regal" posture.
    He might be pictured with an assortment of "attributes" (he
    has some 74 in total), including the trident of his father Shiva,
    representing the three-pronged powers of love, wisdom,
    and action. He might hold a lotus, symbolizing enlighten-
    ment emerging from murky spiritual waters. He has a sacred
    serpent, the Naga, entwined around his body, representing
    kundalini power. He wields a noose to enable the faithful to
    arrest delusion, curb the ego, and restrain passion.

    ✳

    Santa Claus too has a unique sense of personal grooming and
    fashion. He has never cut his white hair or beard, wears small
    round spectacles, and always appears in public wearing the
    same distinctive outfit — a bright red coat with white-fur
    collar and cuffs, white-fur-cuffed red trousers, a cute floppy
    red hat with a white-fur pompon, and a black patent-leather
    belt and boots.

6. **Catchy and Memorable Slogans**
    Ganesha is associated with the respectful chanted mantra:
    "Om Gan Ganpataye Namaha," while Santa Claus is recognized
    by his exuberant: "Ho-ho-ho!"

7. **Unusual Transport**
    Most Hindu gods are assisted by a *vahana*, a Sanskrit term that
    roughly means "celestial vehicle." Ganesha relies on a mouse
    named Musika for assistance. Elephant-headed, large-bodied
    Ganesha can take care of the big life-challenging problems
    people face, but Musika can go into nooks and crannies to
    alleviate the humdrum daily difficulties people encounter.

    ✳

    Santa Claus owns a team of flying reindeer who enable him

to circumnavigate the world at exceptional speed, led by a super-reindeer named Rudolph whose bright red nose illuminates the team's path through harsh winter weather.

8. **Similarly Famous**
    A recent Google search for "Ganesha" yields 1.6 billion hits, while "Santa Claus" generates 1.8 billion hits.

9. **Obscure Wives**
    Ganesha's consorts are not wives in the Western sense, they are personifications of his *shakti*, his creative energy. The number of his wives is uncertain. Depending on which version of the legend you accept, Ganesha is: a) unmarried and celibate, b) has two wives — Buddhi (representing intelligence and wisdom), and Siddhi (spiritual power) — or c) has three wives — Riddhi (prosperity) joins to form a *ménage à quatre*. In the infrequent images in which the wives appear, they are generally shown as smaller figures standing at Ganesha's side. Although created by Lord Brahma specifically because Ganesha was unable to find a bride as wonderful as his mother, none of the wives feature prominently in the Hindu pantheon as independent deities. Without the celebrity status of their famous husband, they would remain in obscurity.

Santa Claus's wife does not have a clear identity. She is generally portrayed as a plump, devoted *hausfrau* who happily stays out of the limelight and supports her husband in his vital work by baking brownies and handling paperwork (obtaining work permits for the elves and replying to correspondence). Several American films have invented names for her — Jessica (in the 1970 film *Santa Claus Is Comin' to Town*), Anya (1985 film *Santa Claus: The Movie*), Margaret (2011 film *Arthur Christmas*), and Ruth (2020 film *Fatman*). None of these names are credible; most Western scholars simply refer to her as Mrs.

Claus (similarly Nordic scholars refer to her by her honorific: Kone, Vaimo, or Maka, depending on their determination of Santa's nationality). I've learned, however, from reliable sources posting in social media, that her close friends, with whom she plays canasta, sips schnapps, and trades cookie recipes, affectionately call her Carol.

10. Global Jet-setters

Both Ganesha and Santa Claus travel huge distances without difficulty. They never get stuck in traffic, have a flight delayed, or have to put up with obnoxious fellow passengers.

In my book *Searching for Ganesha,* I tell a tale about brotherly cunning in the hope of earning a precious reward. In a nutshell: One day a group of gods visited the Shiva-Parvati household and announced that they would present a divine modak containing the nectar of supreme knowledge and immortality to one of their two sons. But there was a condition: "This is a special sweet and must be given only to the wisest and most deserving boy who completes a challenge." "Me, me!" Ganesha and his elder brother Kartikeya cried in unison.

Their mother Parvati would not give in to whining.

"You two can compete for it, like normal children. I'll give the sweet of wisdom to the first son who circumambulates the universe first."

Kartikeya was stronger and faster, and he flew off on his trusty vahana, Parvani, the celestial peacock. Ganesha lounged around the house, ignoring his mother's scolding "since you're not doing anything useful, you might as well clean your room."

After eons and eons, the family got news that Kartikeya was returning. Ganesha, who had been nibbling a mango and watching cricket, calmly got off his ample bum and waddled around his parents three times.

"What on earth are you doing?" his mother asked.

"I'm circumambulating the realm of eternity," he said. "My parents encompass the entire universe. The one we know and all universes yet to be named."

And so, Ganesha won the fraternal competition, and, to this day, is rewarded by offerings of modak.

Santa Claus flies at ridiculous speed to visit every household in the world and leave presents for children. It is thought he is assisted by kind air traffic controllers who clear his path and by local police forces worldwide who do not respond to anxious calls that "a fat, bearded man dressed in red and carrying a big sack is climbing through my neighbor's window."

11. Mysterious Parentage

Ganesha was born through magical incantations and his mother's exfoliated skin.

Santa Claus's parentage is unknown.

12. Isolated, Frigid, Private Homes, Far from the People Who Love Them

While tropical Maharashtra in central India is the most fervent Ganesha stronghold, his original home was with his parents, Shiva and Parvati, in the highest snow-clad mountains of the Himalaya.

Santa Claus lives at or near the North Pole. The exact location is unknown, and at least six countries claim to be his residence. It is not known whether he pays taxes in any of those sites.

13. Both Are Particularly Busy at One Time of the Year

Ganesha is fêted at Ganesha Chaturthi, also called Vinayaka

Chaturthi, a massive 10-day festival usually held in late August to early September during which believers pray to the god and parade majestic statues of Ganesha.

✳

Santa Claus comes into his own … well, you know very well when Santa Claus appears.

14. Ability to Remove Obstacles

A large part of Ganesha's popularity is due to his ability to remove obstacles. His ability is so pronounced that even when Hindus begin to pray to a different god, they first offer a prayer to Ganesha so that he might open the gateway that will assure that the prayer gets through to the designated deity.

✳

Santa Claus is well-known for easily sliding down thin chimneys without harm to person or gifts. In the event no chimney is present, he can stealthily enter and exit any dwelling without causing damage or being noticed.

15. Neither Owns His Own Identity

Ganesha and Santa Claus do not retain any rights to their names, images, or myths. They exist in the public domain. Without copyright or trademark restrictions, artists and marketeers the world over are free to use to use Ganesha and Santa Claus for an unlimited variety of advertising, product names, and legends. Think how much could be achieved if just a tiny royalty for each commercial use of the Ganesha or Santa Claus name, image, or trademark would be paid to a global fund to research cures for children's diseases, alleviate poverty, reverse desertification, safeguard women's rights, and provide pay rises to teachers and health-care workers.

16. Both Have Been Used as Propaganda Symbols for Political Movements

At about the same time, Ganesha and Santa Claus became symbols of powerful political and social movements. We do not know whether they consented to such use of their names and images.

Ganesha played a key role in the Indian independence movement. Bal Gangadhar Tilak (1856-1920) was a prominent leader of the Indian independence movement. He realized that Indians needed to join together and speak with a common voice, but large political gatherings were forbidden by the British East India Company. Tilak, whom the British dubbed The Father of Indian Unrest, understood that Ganesha was loved and worshipped by all castes and classes and could be a unifying symbol for the country. And he knew that while the British could prohibit political protest marches, they could not stop religious gatherings. He channeled the rising patriotic spirit and turned a small, private household Ganesha ceremony into a massive annual Ganesha street festival, now known as Ganesha Chaturthi, celebrated by millions.

In the dark days of the American Civil war, *Harper's Weekly* printed a cartoon of Santa Claus supporting Union forces. The engraving shows Santa, who has arrived in a sleigh, visiting a Union army camp to distribute gifts. He offers the brave soldiers necessities, such as warm socks and copies of the magazine in which the image was published. He entertains the soldiers with a satiric toy jumping jack dangling from a noose, its chest lettered "Jeff" in reference to the Confederate President Jefferson Davis.

In Search of…

THINGS THAT GO BUMP IN THE NIGHT

Lightning Teeth
Help Win a Lover's
Heart and Guarantee an
Election Victory

An Isolated Philippines Island
Has Cornered the Market on
Love Potions and Magical Healing

Paul Spencer Sochaczewski   *Philippine Information Agency*

(Left) Lily Tatong, a Filipina healer, at her roadside amulet stall.
(Right) Governor Orlando "Shane" Fua Jr. Win a heart, win an election.
Everything's possible with the right magic elixir.

SAN ANTONIO, SIQUIJOR ISLAND, THE PHILIPPINES

*W*hat a wonderful world we live in, I thought. For just $10, I could buy a small bottle crammed with a magical potion made out of herbs and scrapings of "lightning teeth." According to Juan Ponce, the elderly traditional healer who created the concoction, the mystical brew will help the bearer entice new lovers. Enjoy business prosperity. Even win a gubernatorial election.

Moving slowly, 97-year-old Ponce showed me a cuspid-shaped chunk of basalt, resembling a prehistoric ax head. "Very rare," Ponce's daughter Tata said. "These lightning teeth mysteriously appear at the base of the tree where lightning has struck."

Juan Ponce's house, in the rural Siquijor village of San Antonio — ground zero for mystical happenings in the Philippines — certainly had the allure of a sorcerer's residence. Set up on a small hill away from the road, his wooden residence and overgrown garden emitted a vaguely uneasy aura in otherwise sunny and tranquil Siquijor Island.

Ponce is one of some 50 *mananambals*, or traditional healers, who live on Siquijor, a half-Singapore-sized island in the center of the Philippines.

Sorcery, magic, and things that go bump in the night are part of Siquijor's allure, along with lovely beaches, a forest reserve, and a down-at-the-heels 19th-century Catholic convent, claimed to be the oldest in Asia.

So important is magic to the island's tourist development, that, at the time I visited, the Siquijor tourism office had proclaimed the destination as "The Mystical Island" (a designation since changed to "The Healing Island"). Mysticism is in the island's DNA — the governor of Siquijor Province, Orlando "Shane" Fua Jr., regularly offers guests small bottles of "love potions" made by either Juan Ponce or Lily Tatong, another *mananambal*.

Juan Ponce suggested that the potions are more than official giveaways. "The governor uses the potions while campaigning," Ponce said, explaining that before the vote that put him in power, Governor Shane, as he is widely called, rubbed a bit of magic elixir into his palm before shaking hands with the electorate.

⚬┄┄┄┄◆┄┄┄┄⚬

At first glance Siquijor, population 87,000, doesn't appear to be a haven of magic arts. It's as laid-back and as verdant as any out-of-the-way Philippines island. Some 70,000 tourists a year stop by, including the Filipino visitors coming for the equivalent of a one-day Magical Mystery Tour and the foreign tourists visiting for the pleasant beaches and excellent scuba diving.

I first visited the island in 2001 with my son David and my friend Bill. I returned in late 2008, accompanied by Abner Bucol, a Siquijor-native and research biologist who works in Silliman University in Dumaguete, an hour's ferry ride from Siquijor.

During our three-day visit, Abner and I visited half a dozen healers, and we quickly learned that there is no fixed route to health in Siquijor.

When we arrived unannounced at Genelou Magsalay Sumalpong's house, she was breast feeding her five-month-old daughter. She lives in a comfortable, but not luxurious concrete house, and like most healers has enough disposable income to afford a nice TV and sound system. My guide Abner explained that he had a cyst on his neck. Sumalpong, 24, listened, examined the cyst and got out her simple equipment. She uses a technique called *bolo-bolo*, onomatopoeic for "blowing bubbles," which detects and removes evil spirits that are causing illness. The key mechanism, she explained after some prompting, is the ordinary-looking oblong black pebble that she put into a water-filled jar. Her grandmother found the stone, "glittering like a crystal egg sitting on a nest," took it home, and put it on the family altar. That night Sumalpong's grandfather had a dream that he would become a *mananambal*, and a family vocation was born. Sumalpong placed the jar against Abner's neck and blew bubbles through a metal straw. The water stayed clear, and she declared that Abner's problem was natural; no devil was involved. Had the water turned murky with dirt, pebbles, and grass, she would have concluded that Abner had been infested by an evil spirit, necessitating an exorcism.

***

Most residents of Siquijor are quick to differentiate between "good" and "bad" mysticism.

Simply put, "good" mysticism, practiced by a *mananambal*, is the stuff of herbal massage, traditional herbal medical healing, love potions, tourist souvenirs of "dragon's teeth" concoctions, heart-shaped carved wooden amulets, and colorful plastic bracelets to protect against, as one dealer suggested, "snake bites, voodoo spells, and vampires."

"Bad" mysticism, practiced by sorcerers, locally called *mama-marang*, is the "dark side," the world of devil-influenced spells. Way back in the isolated hills of Siquijor, people say there are *mama-marang* who turn themselves into animals, talk with the dead and concoct powerful poisons that kill on contact. At least that's the way Josette Armiola of the Siquijor tourist office, who acknowledges she "half-believes" in magic, sees it: "Herbal medicines are good. Witchcraft isn't."

Armiola has a powerful ally in her "good/bad" differentiation — the Catholic Church.

Monsignor Larry Catubig welcomed me to his office next to the ruins of a two-century-old bell tower. He acknowledged that the Church has no problem with healers but does not welcome magicians. I suggested to him that Catholicism, like many religions, is based on miracles. "Yes," he agreed. "Miracles build. But magic destroys."

Pastor Dario Ocay, a Pentecostal pastor of the Blessed Hope Global Outreach, has a more draconian view of traditional healing and its associated magic. Sitting in the cool room that doubles as the church's kindergarten, Ocay said, "It's all the work of Satan, and all healers are demon-possessed." Ocay's worldview is refreshingly black and white. He is an articulate and friendly man (he used to be an encyclopedia salesman), who admits that his father was a sorcerer. "All diseases are caused by demons," he said. "What about something like cancer?" I ask.

"Everyone is a sinner," he answered.

But how bad could the "bad" stuff really be?

Evil enough to kill someone, if Telesforo Lumactod is to be believed.

Abner and I went to his easy-to-find house on the main road

that runs through the commune of Ponong in the hills about half an hour from the slightly busier coastal road. There were no cars, just a few motorized tricycles and motorcycles. Village life went on at its own sleepy tempo — children played, chickens ran around, shopkeepers languidly chased flies from their produce.

Lumactod wore a green golf shirt and blue denim shorts. He is an unimposing Voldemort, with a wispy Van Gogh-style beard and a few missing front teeth. We disturbed him from his afternoon nap, a sensible pastime in the tropics. He was sprawled on a white plastic chair on the front porch of his concrete house, a half-empty bottle of rum close by.

"Yes, I can kill someone," Lumactod said.

Lumactod's modus operandi for mystical mayhem is not as straightforward as, say, Martha Stewart's recipe for apple crumble. His atelier is a secret cave, where he calls up wandering souls. He performs his incantations, aided by a picture of the intended victim or a lock of the person's hair.

I thought for a moment about some truly evil people whom I would like to see injured. I decide to let fate, whatever that might be, take responsibility for their future, and I do not engage Lumactod's services.

I asked whether Lumactod was worried about what will happen to him after he dies.

"I'm already in hell," the 57-year-old man says. But the rum confuses him, and he rambles. "Heaven is only a story. And anyway, God doesn't give me food."

Lumactod also deals in more mundane love potions and concoctions to ensure business success. Could we buy one of his ready-to-use potions? "Come back later," he says, explaining that his wife handles the retail side of the family business. She is a village counselor and had gone to town on official duties.

Call it what you will. Healing. Magic. Mysticism. Hucksterism. The work of the devil or affordable health care? How did Siquijor become Grand Central Station of things that go bump in the night?

Perhaps the early Spanish explorers had a sense of the distinctive personality of Siquijor when they dubbed the island *Isla del Fuego* or "Island of Fire," because it gave off an eerie night-time glow. No matter that this strange light came from the great swarms of fireflies that harbored in the numerous *molave* trees on the island — "Fire Island" has a pleasant metaphysical ring to it.

Vergie Bonocan Miquiabas, a university professor and author of *The Mystical Siquijor in the Philippines*, says one reason for Siquijor's magical positioning is that people are poor and isolated, so they turn to alternative medical healing. "And there are plenty of herbal plants in the forests that provide raw materials for the healers," she says.

Of course, isolation, poverty, and biodiversity occur throughout the Philippines, and other parts of the country have strong metaphysical reputations. But somehow Siquijor has jumped to the front of the queue when people think of magic, and a steady stream of visitors, including high-society matrons and high government officials, seek treatment and protection from Siquijor's practitioners of the grey arts.

Imelda Marcos, the imperious shoe-collecting wife of Philippines President Ferdinand Marcos, was among Siquijor's A-list adherents.

In a generally accepted urban legend, the first lady had a skin disease that resisted treatment by the best Western-trained dermatologists in Manila. She consulted a Siquijor healer who explained that Marcos's disfiguration was caused by a curse placed on her by angry mermen (brothers of mermaids) injured during the construction of the San Juanico Bridge linking Samar and Leyte islands, at the time the longest bridge in the country. This edifice was hailed as a "love bridge," built in honor of the First Lady by her husband. At the urging of a Siquijor healer, Madam Marcos made offerings to the aquatic spirits, and her skin problem cleared up.

(A related popular San Juanico Bridge tale says that the woman in charge of the bridge's construction, annoyed by building delays, consulted a fortune teller who explained the bridge would never be completed unless the blood of children was mixed with concrete to strengthen the foundations. She ordered the bridge laborers to kidnap street children, drain their blood, and throw their bodies into the river. These acts were witnessed by the River Fairy who cursed the woman in charge, causing her legs to grow scales and eternally smell of rotten fish. The bridge's name became a euphemism to describe a form of torture used by military who were ordered by President Marcos to punish political opponents. It involves a person being beaten while the victim's head and feet lay on separate beds and the body is suspended as though to form a bridge.)

Buying amulets in Juan Ponce's home was the rural Philippines equivalent of spiritual fast food — make your choice and take it home. I didn't like it. It was too easy, all cash and no soul. My experience with healers and magicians in Kenya, Madagascar, Indonesia, Thailand, China, and India usually called for at least a cursory discussion of my needs, at least the pretense of giving me something specially concocted for my situation. I found I missed the "personal blessing" aspect of acquiring something mystical. I wanted a human communion, not a retail transaction.

The commercialization of magic in Siquijor extends to the handful of talented illusionists who live on the island.

Arguably the most famous Siquijor conjuror is Vicente Tumala. His home, also on the main drag in San Antonio, is spacious, cool, and comfortable. When Abner and I arrived, a relative was installing a serious stereo system and a bossa nova version of "I could have danced all night" from *My Fair Lady* pounded out the massive speakers, shaking the tin roof.

Up until 2008, Tumala was the David Copperfield of Siquijor. He was much in demand by tourist groups who enjoyed watching him eat burning coals, turning vines into pythons, and making dried, salted anchovies swim.

He's retired now. Tumala became a Charismatic Catholic, he says, and now believes that magic is the work of the devil. And he is still bitter by having been shortchanged by a group of Japanese tourists, who promised him $120 for a "dead-fish-swimming" performance but only gave him $5. It's hard to tell which was the greater reason for his quitting show business — religion or cash flow.

⸺◆⸺

Regardless of the nomenclature — spiritual, supernatural, magic, mystical, or just plain nuts — people around the world put an inordinate amount of faith in talismans, amulets, good luck charms, and magic incantations.

Almost everyone has some superstition or quirk. Knocking on wood to retain good luck. Refusing to walk under a ladder. Changing course when a black cat crosses the path. And who's to say it doesn't work?

⸺◆⸺

I asked whether Juan Ponce used his own concoctions to keep him going. What's his secret?

"Just a glass of rice wine every day," he said.

I tried his rice wine — delicious but headache-inducing in the mid-day sun. But I had a more immediate physical problem than longevity — a chronically stiff lower back. I rubbed on some of Juan Ponce's *haplas* healing oil, which he says is made from some 50 herbs he stores in a giant-sized Johnnie Walker bottle. My back felt better immediately, and the feeling of relief lasted all day.

During a visit to Siquijor a decade ago my son bought a love amulet; a few years later he married a wonderful woman. (I thought of the sound-bite-worthy comments of Monsignor Larry Catubig, who had opined that the best love potion is the way you speak and your money.)

Lily Tatong's daughter, Ferlie, claims empirical proof that her mother's love potions work. "Just look at my four children," she says proudly, as her cute kids scamper around the living room that doubles as a medicinal-bracelet manufacturing center. "Every time I wanted to have a baby I would use this magic bracelet," she said. "With your husband?" I ask gingerly. "No. No need for husbands.

When I need a man, this bracelet is all I need." It was the first time
I had heard of a woman requiring supernatural assistance to get
knocked up.

⸙

But the most eloquent answer I got about whether amulets and
magic potions work came from Siquijor's Governor Orlando "Shane"
Fua Jr., the man whom Juan Ponce suggested used potions to get
elected.

By happy coincidence, on my last day in Siquijor, Abner and
I found ourselves having lunch at a simple open-air restaurant in
the main town. The governor sat at an adjoining table, with several
friends and aides.

I waited until he finished his fish lunch and introduced myself.
After good naturedly blaming journalists for exaggerating the bad
things and ignoring the good, Governor Shane happily talked about
his plans for Siquijor and why people should visit his small province.
Beaches. Nice people. No traffic. Fresh air. Marine nature reserves.
We chatted for 10 minutes, and I sensed he was getting ready to leave
to take care of his gubernatorial duties. "Governor, is it true you
rubbed Juan Ponce's love potion on your hands when you greeted
potential voters?" I asked.

He didn't quite deny it, but he had a comeback that no doubt
he had used previously. "I have something much stronger than any
magic potion," he said. He waited a beat before continuing. "My
personal charm! That's what won me the election."

"Are You Strong Enough to Go Through With This?"

I Make Friends With a Man-Hating Female Vampire Spirit in a City Built on a Ghost Story. She Wants to Follow Me Home. It's My Own Fault.

Paul Spencer Sochaczewski

PBS Digital Studios – Monstrum: Pontianak –
The Vampiric Ghost of Southeast Asia

(Left) Dewi, channeling the Pontianak Farida: "Meester, I'm coming for you."
(Right) The legend of pontianak and kuntilanak ghosts has its stronghold
in modern-day Southeast Asia, particularly Malaysia and Indonesia.
This man-hating spirit is generally associated with tales of young women
who were abandoned by their lovers and died during childbirth.

PONTIANAK, WEST KALIMANTAN, INDONESIA

*T*he shaman asks me a third time. "Are you sure you want to do this?"

I feel like I was back in high school and my soccer coach, Charlie Koch, was looking down the bench to see who he could put into the game. Put me in coach. I can do it. I'm ready.

The shaman, called a *dukun* in Indonesia (and *bomoh* in neighboring Malaysia) was responding to a request I had made hours earlier. I was the first European to pose this particular challenge to the middle-aged man, and he was checking my desire and commitment, and, I suppose, my strength to handle what might take place if he was successful in contacting a man-hating female vampire spirit.

Send me in coach.

For the third time he offers me an easy out. He points to a 30-something woman named Dewi, who was seated nearby, watching quietly.

"She's a medium. She can channel the spirit and you can watch. It'll be easier for you."

But I had come this far and can be stubborn when faced with a challenge. *Put me in coach. I'm sure. I want to speak with a pontianak.*

In the interworld, in the twilight mist of grey rainbows, hovering between dusk and dawn, joy and sorrow, life and death, dwell the ghosts. Wisps of smoke, certainly, but all too real for those who believe.

And the best place in the world to look for ghosts is the western tip of Borneo.

Not just any kind of ghost but a very specific type of spirit that gives this city its name: pontianak. The only city in the world named after a female spirit who is eternally angry at men.

I am in Pontianak. I have visited various shamans over the previous few days and have heard a bunch of pontianak stories. Now I want to "see" one for myself.

A friend found a shaman who was willing to hold a séance and, through a medium, introduce me to a "real" pontianak. The only hitch was that the shaman-for-hire had to pay the medium, buy offerings, and cover his costs. "How much?" I asked. "About $650," my friend said.

Time for plan B.

According to legends, and there are many, a pontianak is a misandrist for good reason: She is the spirit of a woman who died in childbirth, alone, abandoned by the child's father.

The word "pontianak" may be a corruption of the Malay *perem-puan mati beranak* or "young woman who died in childbirth."

She preys on men, indiscriminately. She is pale, dressed in white and horribly ugly, except when she's beautiful. Tip: You can only make a hideous ghost beautiful by hammering a nail into the hole on the nape of her neck; the spirit will then become an attractive and dutiful wife.

The alternative to the expensive séance was provided by my friend Din Osman, a local historian. One rainy afternoon we visited the home of one of his office colleagues, Rustammy. He runs a music café that is attached to his house, and in his home office, I noticed a few electric guitars lying about, like a poor man's Hard Rock Cafe.

Rustammy explained the two options. I could "call" a pontianak myself and have a one-on-one experience with her. Or I could "speak" with a pontianak via Dewi, who was quietly watching our discussion.

We could do it that evening.

"Are you really strong enough?

Send me in coach.

A note on nomenclature (apologies, this gets a bit confusing). In the Malay language, used in Malaysia, Singapore, Brunei, and parts of Indonesia, the term for this particular spirit is pontianak. In the closely related Indonesian language (the difference between the two languages might be compared to the difference between American English and Australian English), the term is kuntilanak. Even though the city of Pontianak is in Indonesia, they use the Malay word, pontianak, for their city and use the Indonesian term, kuntilanak, for the ghost. For simplicity, I will refer to the ghost as pontianak, regardless of whether it appears in Malaysia or Indonesia.

Pontianak has 650,000 people, a large university, shopping malls, traffic jams, and luxury hotels.

And it has a seemingly limitless population of ghosts.

Pontianak probably has more ghosts per capita than any other small city, and virtually everyone I spoke with has a ghost story to tell. It doesn't take long before I imagine the entire town bursting into spirited song — *ooh-ee … one-eyed, one-horned, flyin' purple people eater.*

They're everywhere, and I challenge a visitor to find a town citizen who doesn't have a pontianak story.

Ghosts, sprites, demons, and things that go bump in the night are rampant. *They're in the banana trees. In cellphone towers, in dreams and, most definitely, in schools. And in the soup (don't eat at Auntie Aminah's, she might put a spell on you). There's a particularly nasty pontianak in the old house near the cemetery, where my sister-in-law's ex-boyfriend's motorcycle mechanic's grandfather was killed; just before he died, he ran gibbering into the yard shouting "I'm not the one who killed your baby, go back to your own world."*

My friend Din Osman's story is typical. In 1984 he was riding his motorcycle crossing the bridge over the Kapuas River near the swampy site where the first sultan encountered the ghosts. One end of the bridge also connected with a cemetery. Osman saw a pontianak walking across the span carrying a gravestone. He watched her for a while, then decided that safety was better than curiosity, and he sped away.

Many of the folks I spoke with in Pontianak speculated that the ghosts are spirits of dead women who are stuck between earth and heaven. But beliefs can be slippery. "So you believe it," I would prod. "Not really," each person would reply. "I don't believe in ghosts. But I saw it. I can't explain it. If it's not a ghost, then what is it?"

I met the 10th sultan of Pontianak the evening before the séance. His ancestor was the founder of the city of Pontianak and gave birth to the city's reputation as Ghost Ground Zero.

I was having dinner with two friends who are related to the royal family.

Over the grilled prawns and fish soup, one of my friends, a cousin of the sultan, said, "You're asking so many questions about the royal family, do you want to meet the sultan?"

"But it's already eight-thirty. Isn't it too late?"

"No problem."

So we forgot about dessert, walked to the riverbank, and boarded a comfortable wide-beamed boat that was a semi-permanent café. Rustammy asked the other patrons if they minded a little river cruise, then I handed over a few dollars and the boat untied from the mooring and chugged across the river to the sultan's *kraton* (palace) to meet Syarif Toto Thaha Alkadrie, the 10th sultan, the successor to the man who was Pontianak's first ghost-buster.

In 1771 a prince named Syarif Abdul Rahman al-Gadri, burdened with a dodgy reputation among seafarers and hassled by a vicious ongoing family feud at home, wanted a new start to his life and to settle somewhere without being burdened with the baggage of his past. He sailed along the west Borneo coast and anchored near an empty stretch of land 17 kilometers (10 miles) from the sea where two major rivers meet. It was a strategic place for a settlement, but it had been left empty because it was a swampy jungle believed to be a place of bad spirits — the pontianaks.

Din Osman recounted one of many tales of the founding of Pontianak. He said that for three days and three nights the ghosts mocked the intruders, making an eerie "hee-hee-hee" laughing sound that infuriated Abdul Rahman.

Legend has it Abdul Rahman scared the pontianaks away in the same way he fought his earthly enemies, with a large bombardment of cannons. History is not an exact science here; myth and fact are joined at the hip. Some legends say that the spirits fled. Other myths say that the sultan never got rid of all the ghosts and was haunted for the remainder of his life.

Either way, Abdul Rahman became the first sultan of Pontianak. And the town was given the name it has to this day. Every October 23, the local tourist office celebrates the event with the Pontianak Ghost Festival.

Ten people have assembled in Rustammy's house. Two additional men stroll in.

"Who are you?" Rustammy asks.

"We heard you were going to call a pontianak, and we came over," the strangers say.

Rustammy is annoyed. "I don't know you," he says to the men, angry, but in a polite Indonesian way. "How did you find out about this? Please leave."

Rustammy explains the procedure, what I must do, and what I might expect. Suddenly, one of Rustammy's friends, a man named Andi, starts shouting. His eyes bulge, he arches his back, and pounds the table. "He's a foreigner," the man yells, looking in my direction. "It's not right."

Rustammy doesn't seem too upset. "Ah, that's Datuk Jangut," Rustammy says. "Andi goes into a trance easily. There are so many spirits in this room, and some of them don't want to be bothered. Can you feel them?"

No, I don't feel them. I have attended dozens of séances throughout Indonesia and other parts of Southeast Asia. I've seen men in trances speaking in tongues. Men in trances harmlessly stabbing themselves with knives and broken glass. Men in trances claiming to be my father. One time a man in a trance said he was Moses and wanted me to go to the Middle East to stop the never-ending feud between the Israelis and the Palestinians.

Rustammy calmly tells the spirit that we aren't going to bother anybody, so just settle down and be cool. Datuk Jangut (the Bearded Lord) leaves Andi's body without another word.

When an AirAsia flight from Surabaya to Singapore disappeared in late 2014, Jakarta Governor Basuki "Ahok" Tjahaja Purnama referred to the high density of ghosts and mystical phenomena in the region of Kalimantan, where the plane was thought to have crashed. He joked that *jinn* (supernatural creatures in Islamic mythology; origin of the English genie) might be responsible for the disappearance of the plane. His statement was poorly received.

⸻ ◆ ⸻

Too many people. Four of us go into an adjacent room, partly enclosed.

"You're really sure you are strong enough to see a pontianak?"

Yes, coach.

"Sit in a lotus position, close your eyes, and call the pontianak," Rustammy instructs.

I'm not comfortable sitting in a lotus position; I sit against a wall.

"Hold your hands out in front of you."

Which I do.

"Close your eyes."

Which I do.

"Now call the pontianak."

Which I do. Do I need to say it out loud or to myself? I opt for a silent murmur. *Hello Ibu Pontianak! Good day to you. Miz Pontianak, where are you? I know you're here. Come to me. I want to see you.*

"She's close, I can feel she's close," Rustammy says.

"Order her to come."

Get your vampire ass over here right now.

"She's right here," Rustammy insists. "I can feel her."

I don't feel her.

"Order her to come," Rustammy says, insistent that his tactics will work.

I'm not sure that it's a good idea to boss around a female vampire ghost who hates men.

I mix the strategies of command and request. *Come closer, Madam Pontianak. Close to me, close to you. I order you. I command you. You're close. I want to see you.*

And then my monkey-mind kicks in. I start to hum the Carpenters' song "Close to You." *Why do birds suddenly appear, every time, you are near?*

I want to giggle.

Do pontianaks have a sense of humor? Do they appreciate music of the '70s?

After about five additional minutes of unanswered entreaties and scraps of banal earworm music, I open my eyes. "Nothing," I say.

The discipline of ghost taxonomy is still in its infancy, and the spiritual world could certainly use someone like Swedish botanist Carl Linnaeus, who was to taxonomy what Brigitte Bardot was to the bikini.

One might argue that nature (and the spirit world), by definition, is chaotic and disorderly. But Linnaeus, who liked to say, "God created, Linnaeus organized," strove for structure and logic; he was frustrated by the descriptive chaos of mushrooms. Some were tasty, some were hallucinogenic, and some would kill you. True, they were all mushrooms but not alike. Same-same but different. In the early 18th-century Linnaeus lamented that there was no common, easy-to-use, universal system of nomenclature for different species, citing the case of the common tomato that he noted was confusingly described as *Solanum caule inermi herbaceo, foliis pinnatis incises, racemis simplicibus* — the solanum with the smooth stem that is herbaceous and has incised pinnate leaves.

In his book *The Malaysian Book of the Undead*, Danny Lim has tried to put similar order into ghost taxonomy, cataloguing 126 different types of ghosts, vampires, hantus, demons, were-tigers, evil spirits, goblins, and other creatures you don't want to meet on a dark and stormy night. Malaysia has plenty of faults, but you gotta love a nation with enough ghosts for more than 10 football teams.

Like a taxonomist, Lim suggests various classifications:

- The "class of disease-causing ghosts," like *hantu cika*, which causes colic, or *hantu sawan*, which causes convulsions (*sawan*) in young children.
- Nature spirits that inhabit snakes, rivers, and wind.
- Men who turn themselves into were-tigers, were-pigs, and

were-crocodiles.
- A conservation spirit, *hantu songkei*, that opens snares "to release trapped animals."
- One ghost that takes up a large space in the Malaysian/Indonesian psyche is *orang minyak*, "greasy man," who is a slippery take on the Hunchback of Notre Dame; he wanders around naked and covered in oil, and preys on beautiful young women.

⸎

But the female ghosts steal the show.

The pontianak is the most prominent of a large sisterhood of feminine spirits who are descended from women who have been abused by men and have died in childbirth. Gather some Malaysian or Indonesian friends and ask them to name and describe the characteristics of the various angry female ghosts. There is considerable overlap and confusion. They are beautiful and entice young men to messy demises. They are old hags with droopy breasts. Or they exhibit both personas, depending on the situation and who's telling the story.

Here are some of the more well-known forms of angry female Malay ghosts identified by ghost taxonomists; they are variations on a single theme, just as the beagle, the Siberian husky, and the Yorkshire terrier are all *Canis lupus familiaris*:
- The classic female vampire ghost is called *pontianak* in Malaysia and *kuntilanak* or *matianak* in Indonesia. She is the ghost of a woman who died in childbirth and sucks the blood of men who have wronged her.
- *Sundel bolong* is the spirit of a woman who has been raped and abandoned to die. She has a deep hollow in her back. Very nasty piece of work.
- *Langsuir* has the ability to fly like a pontianak. She is sometimes associated with the owl, called "ghost bird" in Malay.
- *Hantu tetek*, also known as *hantu kopek*, is a huge old hag with pendulous breasts, who preys on children, thereby encouraging kids to get home in time for *maghrib* (sunset prayer) or risk

being captured by her and smothered to death. Many cultures have this kind of scary big momma witch; the tale of Hansel and Gretel comes to mind.

- *Churel* is another female ghost with sagging breasts, a consistent feature of their ilk. And like other female ghosts, she can also appear as a beautiful young woman who can charm any man. Because young men caused her death during childbirth, the churel drinks their blood, beginning with the man she loved in life. There are numerous ways to get rid of a churel, including burning a ball of thread along with a just-deceased body in the belief that the woman's spirit will be so preoccupied with unwinding the ball that she won't bother to haunt anyone still alive.

- *Penangallan* is described by Danny Lim as having "long flowing hair, penetrating red eyes, and a long protruding tongue. She feeds on human blood and flesh, with a preference for the taste of a newborn infant. When she goes out on the town, she is able to separate her head and organs from the rest of her body, which she leaves in a container of vinegar to preserve it until she returns." As Lim says, "A woman smelling of vinegar is not to be trifled with." This head-and-intestines creature seeks houses where women are about to give birth. The way to prevent her entry is by hanging pineapple or pandan thorns around the house; the sharp points will hook the penangallan's flailing intestinal tracts and entrap the spirit.

"You were so close," Rustammy says. Like a manager talking to a baseball batter who hits a long ball that is caught when the outfielder makes a spectacular leaping catch.

But actually, I wasn't close at all. I don't believe in this stuff.

"Want to try again?"

Rustammy instructs me to relax and extend my arms. "Ask the pontianak to shake your hands."

I've done this type of thing before. The power of suggestion is a strong power indeed. I hold my hands in front of me, keeping them still. *Come on pontianak, make my hands jiggle.*

I sit there for another few minutes. Nothing. I stop murmuring and speak loudly. I order the spirit to come to me, to make my hands shake. I command her in English. In Indonesian. In French. In Thai. I run out of languages. Oh yeah, German. That must be a good language for ordering a spirit to come hither. *"Komm sofort her."* No, make it stronger. *"Sonst,"* I order with menace in my voice.

And just for fun I start to wiggle my hand.

Once the wiggling starts, the jiggle and jangle of my hands became stronger and my arms are bouncing around, like a small boat on a rough sea. But I am in control. I could stop it at any moment, but it is sort of fun. Let's see how this plays out.

I'm speaking clearly. "Come to me. I order you. I humbly request you. Sorry to impose, but I'm only in Pontianak for a short time and it's now or never. I have a story to write."

What a great song Burt Bacharach wrote for Karen and Richard Carpenter.

Karen Carpenter couldn't be a pontianak. Could she? No, no way.

Monkey mind goes wild. I'm shaking my arms and having a good old time.

Foreplay but no climax. No ghost appears. After a few more minutes, I deliberately stop my flailing arms, take a breath, and open my eyes.

⁂

We take a break. As we rejoin the group, Rustammy's wife, Anni, who had been drinking tea and chatting with friends, becomes possessed. She doesn't shout, but her eyes roll up in their sockets and she is quietly sick. The spirits are up and about, targeting impressionable women.

Just as Westerners are taught the Heimlich maneuver, most Indonesians seem to know how to ask a spirit to leave. Someone puts his hand on Anni's forehead, mumbles Islamic prayers, and "sweeps" away the spirit. Anni is an elegant woman, wearing a dress with a Burberry-style plaid. She calms down, a bit embarrassed by

121

the mess she has made.

———◆———

And then, Dewi, the quiet housewife in the maroon headscarf sitting opposite me, lets out a shriek that, excuse the cliché, could have woken the dead. It is a cinematic screech, worthy of the best (or the worst, it's hard to tell sometimes) pontianak movies. Her voice goes all husky; she lets out a high-pitched "ha-hee-ha-hee" laugh of maleficence that could equally be a cry of anguish.

Her voice can best be described by a phrase I would never allow my writing students to use: blood-curdling. Laughter. Screaming. Crying. Sobbing. "You people are bothering me," she cries out. Her gaze is distant and unfocused, her eyes hooded, her voice husky. Repeat laughter, screaming, crying, sobbing.

Dewi starts to shake, jerks around and stands up. Her headscarf goes flying. It looks like she is having an epileptic fit. Softer laugh. "Blood. See the blood!?" she shrieks.

Dewi quiets down a bit. Rustammy speaks to her, asks who she is.

"Farida," she spits out. "My name is Farida. I was killed by a man. I want to go to Meester Paul. He called me."

Meester Paul. That's me.

"I want blood. His blood." Laughter and sobbing. "I want to return. Don't bother me." Dewi crawls into the next room, her sobbing mixed with a hysterical laugh.

Rustammy calms her down. "Go back. It's okay, Farida. Go back."

Then Dewi erupts again. "I was torn apart. I'll remember his face forever. I don't want to go home. I want to follow Meester."

Dewi collapses. She is lying on her back. She looks like she is in a coma.

Rustammy "wipes" her body to remove the ghost. It's a cleansing action in which he rapidly sweeps the negative energy from Dewi's head, her back, her stomach, her legs. Even Western massage therapists know this move.

After a few minutes Dewi opens her eyes and sits up. We all breathe easier.

Wherever there are ghosts there are surely ghostbusters.

A dukun has to know not only how to call a spirit but, more critically, how to get rid of one.

My friend Amalia is a Singaporean spirit guide who makes a good living flying around the world cleansing homes and businesses of bad spirits for Beverly Hills-types. You would recognize the names of some of her clients.

At the village level as well, folks like Rustammy "cleanse" the man or woman who has been bothered by evil spirits. Whether the demons are of our own creation or unwelcome intruders, the shaman helps us cleanse our souls. We all tango with our demons, weaving, posturing, conquering and submitting, seducing and some-times conquering. Demons are our dark sides, our uncontrollable desires, our malicious thoughts and actions.

Vampire movies sink their teeth into cinema-goers in most countries. A quick check of the IMDb database gives some 200 results with "vampire" in the title, including *Jesus Christ Vampire Hunter*, *Vampire Hookers*, *I Bought a Vampire Motorcycle*, and *A Polish Vampire in Burbank*.

Pontianak- and kuntilanak-themed films have been box-office favorites in Malaysia and Indonesia since 1958 when the Malaysian film *Anak Pontianak* (Child Pontianak) was released, followed three years later by the Indonesian film *Kuntilanak*. A spate of female vampire ghost films ensued, followed by a three-decade hiatus. The industry picked up again in the 2000s.

L. Krishnan, one of the pioneers of the Malaysian film industry is in his 90s and lives in Thailand. His films include some of the classic Malaysian ghost films, such as the 1958 *Serangan Orang Minyak* (Attack of the Orang Minyak).

"No, I don't believe in ghosts, but the people who go to the cinema do," he explained over lunch at a Bangkok café. "There were times when the film was shown in a cinema, and the film burned because the projectionist hadn't said the proper prayers."

Shankar Punjabi is another leading horror film director who doesn't believe in ghosts. "No, I've never seen a ghost, and I never got possessed," he said. "If you believe in ghosts, you will see them. It's the power of suggestion. They go into self-induced trances. Imagination works best in a dark room. If you believe, you will feel; if you feel, you will see."

Over coffee in a Jakarta restaurant, Indonesia-based Shankar added: "But I've had actors who got possessed, and we always have an *ustaz* [Islamic spiritual teacher] on call during the shoot to treat the crew and actors who get possessed."

Prem Pasha, a Malaysian filmmaker who is L. Krishnan's son, recalled that when he was about seven he visited the set of his father's film, being shot at night at an old English bungalow in Kuala Lumpur. "I remember that Noordin Ahmad, the star who played the orang minyak, approached the camera," Prem said. "I looked up and saw a 'real' orang mnyak watching the proceedings from the balcony where Noordin had just come from."

Teenage boys like to tempt fate, and when Prem was 16, he and two friends went to a cemetery to spend the night. He doesn't remember the details, but they were approached by a woman who glowed, like she was covered in diamonds. Prem went into a coma for two days, and when he awoke, he was suffering a high fever and his frantic grandmother was rubbing Indian holy ash on his forehead.

I asked if they had called a bomoh. "No, ninety-nine point nine percent of bomohs are fakes," he said. "But what about spirits and ghosts?" I asked. "Ah they're real."

Are the pontianak films sexist? Malaysian Glen Goei, who, with Gavin Yap, is writing a new pontianak film, thinks they represent the 1950s Malaysian society when men and women knew their roles. I'm not suggesting he thinks this, but the extension of this idea is that in rural Malay societies women are closer to the spiritual world than men; they have special, often nasty, powers, and are fickle about whom they choose to befriend and elect to curse. Perhaps this is male resentment (or acknowledgement) that Malay women, like women throughout most of Asia, bear the brunt of the labor, assume a large chunk of familial responsibility, and are often the stronger and more reliable of the two genders.

I had coffee with ghost-taxonomist Danny Lim in Kuala Lumpur. Lim agrees that ghost stories and films reflect rural village life. "You don't have many urban ghosts," he says, although some modern ghost films feature sophisticated urban men (usually spoiled playboys and arrogant businessmen) encountering traditional spirits.

I wanted to speak with an actress who played a vampire ghost. I was introduced to Julia Perez by a mutual friend, a leading Indonesian film producer. I was in Jakarta, and she was in a Singapore hospital. I was surprised she bothered to exchange text messages with me to set up a phone interview. The day before our talk, she had undergone an operation for cervical cancer.

Known by her nickname Jupe (pronounced Joo-Pay), her career has risen due largely to her energetic portrayal of a range of sexy and nasty ghosts. She has starred in some of the most famous Indonesian kuntilanak films such as *Jeritan Kuntilanak* (Scream of the Kuntilanak), *Kuntilanak Kesurupan* (Trance of the Kuntilanak), *Kuntilanak Kamar Mayat* (The Mortuary Ghost), and *Beranak Dalam Kubur* (Birth in the Graveyard).

"Acting in a horror movie is not difficult," Jupe says. "They're the same as any action movie."

But has she seen ghosts while making her films?

"Not clearly, not in front of my face, but I've seen strange shadows. My grandmother told me they exist."

I didn't know how hard to push a woman who had just had major surgery, but I asked whether she believed in these spirits.

"I believe fifty percent. There are mystical things we have to respect. But the other fifty percent is just human behavior."

How can you recognize a pontianak? And, more important, what can you do when you are confronted by one?

The presence of a pontianak can sometimes be detected by a sweet floral fragrance identifiable as that of the plumeria, followed by an awful stench.

A pontianak kills her victims by digging into their stomachs with her sharp fingernails and devouring their sex organs. If you have your eyes open when a pontianak is near, she will suck them out of your head. Pontianaks locate prey by sniffing out clothes left outside to dry, and some people refuse to leave any article of clothing outside of their residences overnight.

And most insidious, the pontianak announces her presence through baby cries. If the cry is loud, then the ghost must be far away. If the baby's cry is soft, then she is close, ready to punish a man. It doesn't really matter to the pontianak whether the man she has targeted is good or evil; all men are the same, which is to say all men, according to her definition, deserve to die.

———◆———

I kneel down next to Dewi and ask if she had any recollection of what had just happened. And she goes wild. It is a false calm. Farida has not left at all, but was lying in wait, like a hibernating bear. Dewi screams and sobs and laughs. This time she looks straight at me. "I want to follow you. You follow me to the cemetery."

She picks up a plastic water bottle and throws it across the room.

Dewi holds out her hand. She wants me to take it so she can guide me to the cemetery. I refuse. Her eyes bulge, unfocused. "Meester," she says, using the expression Indonesians in an earlier generation used to address Dutchmen. "Meester. You called me. I am Farida. You wanted to see me. I am here for you."

———◆———

Why do ghost stories linger in so many countries?

Some people feel the pontianak is an enforcer of morality, a creation of wives who wanted to discourage their husbands from engaging in casual sex with women they might meet on the road at night. Be faithful, the man is told, and he won't have any supernatural complications.

Dimas Jayasrana is an Indonesian film producer who thinks that an encounter with a ghost is like meeting a superstar. "Seeing an old lady in a white dress who is dripping blood and laughing like a little girl is the village equivalent of running into George Clooney," he said. And, Dimas adds, ghosts are useful for disciplining kids. All cultures have tales of ogre-like beings. In the English-speaking world, we are told "be good, or the bogeyman will get you." The bogeyman, so feared by young children, is another scary Indonesian creation that was inspired by the Bugis, a race of Indonesian seafarers (and sometimes aggressive pirates) of whom the British colonials developed a healthy fear.

***

Dewi crawls into the next room, knocks over a table with coffee cups, then crashes into a computer printer. She huddles in a corner, then squats on a chair.

I don't get too close to her. But she approaches me. "MEEE-ster-rrr," she says, rolling her Rs in a supernatural vibrato, drawing out the two-syllable word for several seconds. "MEEE-Sterrrr. You called me. Fifteen years. I am Farida. You called me."

Fifteen years? I have no idea if that was her age when she died or how long she's been in this place between two worlds.

Dewi then ignores me, like a small child who's bored with a toy. She shudders, and Rustammy goes to her to cleanse her once again.

***

The pontianak is an equal-opportunity ghost. In multi-cultural Malaysia, where Malays, Chinese, and Indians live side-by-side but not always tension-free, pontianaks traverse racial, religious, and urban/rural divides.

Pontianaks have, so far, escaped the scrutiny of the Islamic fundamentalists in Malaysia. These are the fun-killing folks who have outlawed Halloween because it's both too Christian and too pagan. This dress-up holiday is "associated with the devil" and is "clearly contrary to the values of Sharia," according to the National Fatwa

Council, Malaysia's top Islamic body.

Perhaps because pontianaks are home-grown, they are socially acceptable. As cultural observer Amir Muhammad writes in the forward to *The Malaysian Book of the Undead*, by Danny Lim, "The ghosts we choose to believe in can also say a lot about our attitudes towards gender, the natural environment, and even race."

⸻◆⸻

Rustammy brings Dewi out of the trance, and this time it seems like Farida has genuinely left.

"So, you saw a pontianak," Rustammy says to me.

"But she didn't come when I called her myself," I say.

"But that's exactly what did happen. You called her," Rustammy says, "and she came to you, through Dewi. You saw Farida. She'll be with you tonight."

I think about that for a moment: "Never mind, that's ok. I got what I came for."

And Rustammy gets really pissed off: "But you called her. She came. You have a deal."

Now my monkey mind recalls the story "The Devil and Daniel Webster." I don't have a valid contract with a pontianak. Or do I?

Of course, I don't believe all this stuff. But I also don't want to insult my hosts by appearing to not take it seriously. "What can we do?"

Rustammy obviously is disappointed in my lack of commitment. "You're not convinced, I can see that. But still, you called her, and she came."

And so?

"Chicken blood should do the trick."

I look bewildered. Rustammy explains: "She wants your blood. But she'll settle for chicken blood."

It is about midnight on a Sunday night. We are in a middle class, residential neighborhood of Pontianak. You can't just go into the backyard and grab a chicken. And the live chicken market is surely closed.

But this is Indonesia, and everything is possible. I dig into my wallet and give a few bills to a young man. Forty-five minutes later he comes back with an unhappy-looking red chicken strapped to his motorcycle handlebars.

"Do I need to kill it myself?" I ask.

"No, since you're not a true believer, we can do it. You can go home."

I don't like the religious connotation of whether I am a "believer," but perhaps I am overreacting.

To be certain, I ask one last time. "So, this will satisfy Farida and keep her happy?"

"It should be okay. She probably won't bother you tonight," Rustammy says. "But you never know."

It's not hard to see how the guided trance state of a pontianak séance uses similar dynamics to some religions and cults. "Do you believe?" Do you *really* believe? Do you want the Holy Spirit to enter you and save you? Like *Ulysses'* Molly Bloom, you spurt out "Yes! Yes! Yes!" Then comes speaking in tongues, fainting, signing over the mortgage to your house, and dancing with rattlesnakes. A true believer is born.

I return to my comfortable hotel around one in the morning, take a shower, and hop into bed. I have no fear that a pontianak has followed me home. I don't believe in such stuff. I turn the air-con up and snuggle in for a good rest.

Just as I am hitting that never-never land between consciousness and sleep, I hear a faint sound that jars me awake. I listen more carefully. It is the cry of a baby. Unmistakable. Coming from the next room. Damn, that meddling pontianak Farida did follow me home.

And then I remember that earlier in the day I had heard a baby crying in the adjoining room. Parents travelling with a young child — so common in Indonesia as not to be worth a second thought. Surely that is the baby's cry that I hear. Of course, it isn't a pontianak. Surely not. Just a normal human baby crying for a feeding. Isn't it?

THE GRANDMOTHER WHO SPITS AT GHOSTS

The Guardian

Pontianaks, such as the ones Maya Satrini encountered, frequently inhabit forests. The spirits told her she should not talk to me; Maya disagreed. They spat. Maya spat. Maya won.

Maya Satrini doesn't look like a woman who could beat up a pontianak.

She's a thin, neat, serious grandmother who lives in Singkawang, a small city two hours north of Pontianak.

But Maya has steel in her character.

She runs a non-governmental organization that tries to stop the trafficking of women from the region to gangs in Hong Kong, Taiwan, and Malaysia. "Young girls from the villages are promised jobs as maids or think they're going to get married," she explained, but often they wind up as "family whores," forced to service many men. They're promised salaries, but they receive nothing after the down payment of a few hundred dollars. Eventually they get HIV and are sent back. "Sometimes I get a call in the middle of the night," Maya explains, "to rescue a girl left on the side of some rural road."

Maya believes the origin of the pontianak myth is based on the widespread (and not incorrect) belief that men don't take responsibility for fatherhood.

The first sultan of Pontianak encountered pontianaks when

he wanted to make a settlement in the swampy forest. Similarly, Maya's house abuts a forest, and she thinks that could be one reason why her son and two grandchildren saw pontianaks in front of the family home — it's common knowledge that such a wilderness is the haunt of demons.

"Pontianaks are spirits which haven't had a chance to settle," she says, explaining that most people die because their contract with Allah is finished. "But some spirits don't go back to Allah immediately; they're waiting for a promise that has yet to be kept."

Several pontianaks appeared to Maya a few days before my visit. "It was eight-thirty in the morning," she recalls. "I was in my bedroom. They looked like normal adult women, except I could see through them — they were transparent."

"One of the ghosts was angry with me," Maya told me. "She knew you were coming and said I mustn't talk with you, that you had no business delving into such things."

Maya said that she told the ghost that they had no such agreement and told the spirit to leave.

And then the pontianak spit at her.

Maya's face became red, and a rash immediately appeared.

Maya spit back. "The pontianak's face became red, and her eyes looked like they would burst out of her head," Maya recalled.

The ghosts disappeared. Maya treated her rash, which she described as being "like a bee sting," with an herbal remedy made of charcoal, garlic, onion, and dried chili. The swelling went away after 15 minutes.

ON THE YETI TRAIL
Heading to the Mountain Where the Elusive Creatures Have Been Sighted

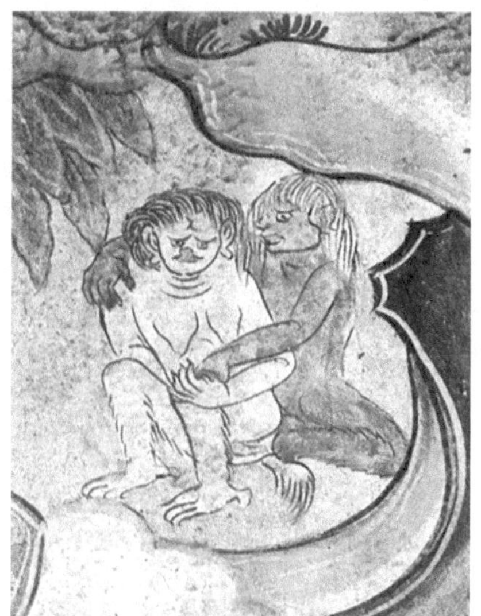

Paul Spencer Sochaczewski
The yeti couple hidden in a corner of the temple at
Ogyen Choling, central Bhutan.

OGYEN CHOLING, TANG VALLEY, BHUTAN

"*I*f you want to look for a yeti, just climb the mountain behind the village. That's where they've been sighted."

I was enjoying a post-dinner whiskey with Kunzang Choden and her husband, Walter Roder, at their home in the Tang Valley in central Bhutan. The talk had drifted into yeti tales. Kunzang's comment that yetis "have been sighted" caused me to pause. The logical part of my brain remembered the days when I was a teenager on a modest allowance buying Roman coins. Some dealers offered bulk lots of a hundred battered coins, with the tantalizing salesman's come-on: "Gold has been found in lots like this."

More enticing was Kunzang's admonition: "Just climb that mountain." It was a refrain I've heard elsewhere in Asia; when I was searching for tiger magicians or small people of the forest, I was frequently told, "you can find the strange wonders you're searching for over the next hill, beyond the next mountain." Just keep walking, cross the raging river, never stop imagining.

On the other hand, this was Bhutan, an isolated Himalayan country with a cultural mythology as rich as the biodiversity in its extensive forests. Bhutan is prime yeti habitat. Kunzang herself, who grew up in this rural valley, wrote a book titled *Bhutanese Tales of the Yeti*, so she has both a local knowledge of things that go bump in the night as well as a Western logical education to help her put strange happenings into perspective.

❖

I needed a long, hard walk.

For the past several days I had been helping my wife photograph temple murals for her PhD dissertation at Kunzang Choden's Ogyen Choling estate. My eyes were beginning to spin with images of bodhisattvas with unpronounceable names and convoluted mythologies.

And then there was a rare mandala of Shambhala, the mythical "pure land" that is the origin of the Western concept of Shangri-la. I could see how an adept could reach a higher plane by meditating on the painting's spiritual geometry. Always hope for a better tomorrow, provided you believe strongly enough today.

So many tales, so many Big Ideas in this holy place.

Most of the pictures were hard to photograph. They were painted on canvas and shiny. The available light was a mixture of harsh sunlight mixed with deep shadow, with the added complication of irregularly placed overhead fluorescent lights. Also, some of the smaller images were hidden behind curtains or in dark corners and could only be photographed by setting up a makeshift scaffold and lighting the small area to be photographed. We estimated we had looked carefully at perhaps half of the painted images that needed to be catalogued. Each day brought a surprise. It was like looking at the world's biggest "Where's Waldo" illustration or really paying attention to Hieronymus Bosch's "Garden of Earthly Delights."

I suffer from Stendhal's syndrome — I get a headache after spending too much time in the presence of overwhelmingly beautiful and important artwork. I needed some fresh air, broader horizons. A search for my own obscure treasures. Some yeti-hunting, a tough walk "up the mountain," was just what I wanted.

What is the allure of a mirage, a wisp, a legend?

Why are people so fascinated by the yeti?

Is it because they mirror our dark side, and in the process, help define us as human?

Kunzang gave me a crash course in yeti-ology.

"There are countless stories about the *migoi*," she said, using the Bhutanese name for the yeti.

They're not people.

They're not animals.

They're deities and spirits that can manifest as yetis, creatures with supernatural powers.

They are territorial and don't like intruders in their wilderness domain.

They can be dangerous. Or not.

They can make themselves invisible.

"Oh, there's one other distinctive feature. The adult females always have long droopy breasts. They flip them over their shoulders when they run." Kunzang's tip: If you are in the wilds of Bhutan and happen to be attacked by a migoi, take a moment to determine its gender. If it's female, run downhill — she will trip over her pendulous breasts, and you will be able to escape her clutches. If the migoi is male, run uphill, through undergrowth. His incredibly long penis will drag on the ground and get caught in low-growing bushes.

In popular Western culture, Nepal gets most of the yeti media coverage. But Bhutan can also stake its claim to being a yeti stronghold.

Hearty trekkers can tackle the difficult Snowman Trek hiking trail in the high Himalayas in the north of the country.

Bhutan is the only country that has created a national park to protect the yeti. This is a place in which I have trekked, the Merak-Sakteng National Park in the east of the country. Good people, lovely scenery, not a yeti in sight.

And it is arguably the only country to be home to both a large high-mountain yeti and a mini-yeti, called *mechume* or *mirgola*, a meter-tall ape-like creature that lives in the dense forests of larch, bamboo, and rhododendron.

For the climb to the "yeti sighting place," at a location called Khramai, I was accompanied by our guide Karma Wangdi, 61, and a local farmer named Tashi Phuntso, 39. After about an hour of setting off, Tashi's dog Norsangla decided to join us. Tashi had left him behind, but Norsangla, four, obviously had felt that he wanted to be part of our adventure.

The path kept climbing. I stopped a few times to take some deep breaths of the clear air. For Tashi, it was a walk in the park. It was a workout for Karma Wangdi, a village boy who grew up in an adjacent valley but who has lived years in the cushier environment of Thimphu, Bhutan's capital. For me, it was a boy's adventure. About halfway up, I could see our destination, a large building perched on the edge of an outcrop. It didn't look that far away.

Tashi, who has lived in the village his entire life, said he had seen a migoi a few years earlier. It was a rainy morning, and he had gone to help his mother care for the yak herd. Lingering nearby was a migoi, who sauntered off when it saw Phuntso approach. Phuntso showed us the field where the encounter had taken place.

I had never met a village dog as zen-like as Norsangla. He was a big, black, and tan mountain dog, with one brown eye and one blue. Most Bhutanese village dogs are fierce. Norsangla, whose name means "good wishes," never barked. He was as gentle as a suburban golden retriever and liked to have the back of his ears scratched. I dare say, his was an "old soul."

But I wasn't sure that having Norsangla around was good for our yeti search. If a yeti came calling, would Norsangla break his silence and scare off the yeti? Or would the yeti sense that this placid animal was an easy midnight snack and invade our camp?

There are two schools of thought about what entices/disgusts a yeti. "To attract a yeti, burn plastic and rubbish," Kunzang said. "They are sensitive to bad smells and will become angry that someone is polluting their neighborhood and come to investigate."

I liked the idea of an eco-conscious yeti, but other folks told me the opposite.

"No, better to burn sweet-smelling pine, juniper, and herbs," Karma said. He had accompanied us from Thimphu but grew up on a farm in an adjacent valley. "They are attracted to homely, natural smells."

Ditto for personal hygiene. One expert said I should not bathe and must hang around barnyard yaks for a few days. Another self-declared expert, however, recommended deodorant and flossing.

The biggest quandary potentially faced by a yeti-hunter is what do you do if you find one?

A true scientist would say that's no quandary at all. You hit it with a tranquillizer dart and do the needful. No tranquilizer gun? Well, you shoot the thing. Because unless you have one on the lab table, all you have is a Grand Wisp of Lofty Expectations.

But most yeti-chasers wouldn't pull the trigger.

I attribute this reticence to two concerns:

The first is that the yeti is so close to being human that killing one would be a form of homicide.

The second is that most yeti-chasers don't want the animal to be found. They don't want the yeti to be autopsied and have its skull measured, its hair and blood analyzed, its stools dissected, or its DNA put through an expensive techno-gadget that would tell us how close the animal is to us, and vice versa. Most serious yeti-chasers claim they prefer to live with the myth, although my cynical side feels that this keep-the-myth-alive attitude might simply be the rationalization of researchers who failed in capturing the beast.

⟵———◆———⟶

People strive for the light. Moths to the flame.

But even the brightest, most enlightened individual has a shadow.

Our dark side — violent, arrogant, spiteful, fearful — is something we try to overcome. Some people seek religion. Some turn to meditation. Others engage in merit-making and doing good works. And some people couldn't give a damn and carry on, business as usual.

Jung called this dark side of the soul the "shadow."

Some Asian religions call this "ignorance," and temples and morality tales are rich in illustrating the idea that one of the main job descriptions of the gods, and hence of mortal men, is to subdue the mischievous Demon of Ignorance.

Do yeti stories evolve from this recognition of the duality of the soul? So much Asian philosophy is based on managing opposites. To get crops to grow, you need both the rainy season and the sunny season. We exist in a cycle of life and death. The world runs on an endless dynamic of polarities: male and female, exploration and nurturing, day and night, good and evil.

The Balinese, who (with some justification) consider themselves a highly evolved society, file the pointed cuspids of children to modify "animal teeth." In other parts of Indonesia, babies are not allowed to crawl on the floor, lest they develop animal-like characteristics. No matter how poor you are, you try to be presentable, with good (or at least clean) clothes and socially approved deportment. No wonder many traditionally educated Asians shake their heads when they encounter loud, rude Westerners. Asians can be both appalled and curious when they see men who wear backward baseball caps and put their shoe-encased feet on beds and furniture. And let's not mention what emotions are stirred when Asians see Western women wearing scanty outfits when visiting temples or post nude selfies while climbing sacred volcanoes. (Though to be fair, plenty of contemporary Asians take rudeness and bad behavior to impressive levels; arrogance and bad manners are not the sole domain of Westerners. A curse on all their ill-mannered houses.)

The yeti is not human. But it's a disturbingly close reverse image, like looking at ourselves in a darkened mirror. The yeti is Caliban, close enough to ourselves to make us wonder what this business we call humanity is all about.

You define yourself partly by what you are not.

As William Butler Yeats wrote in "The Second Coming:"

Turning and turning in the widening gyre

The falcon cannot hear the falconer

Things fall apart; the centre cannot hold;

Mere anarchy is loosed upon the world,

The blood-dimmed tide is loosed, and everywhere

The ceremony of innocence is drowned.

The best lack all conviction, while the worst

Are full of passionate intensity.

Could the "wild men" have an atavistic link with wild beasts encountered when our pre-human ancestors overlapped with other hominids?

Harry Marshall, a British filmmaker who has made documentaries on the yeti, orang pendek, and related creatures for BBC and National Geographic, says:

"We know that our Homo sapiens ancestors overlapped with other hominids, that they mated and produced viable offspring, of which we are the proof. Our genome, with its small but significant percentages of Neanderthal and Denisovan (and who knows what else) DNA is evidence of this hybridization. I believe the parable of Esau and Jacob — the smooth man and the hairy man — is an allegory of how our ancestors usurped the birthright — or more simply, ethnically cleansed their world of the other hominids we once shared the planet with. I think it's an extraordinary part of who we are and genetics is finally going to reveal the extent of our involvement with and debt to the hairy other."

In 1952, while climbing in the Cho Oyu region of the Himalayas, Sir Edmund Hillary, one of the first two men to have climbed Mount Everest, found a scrap of skin covered in blue-black fur and was told by his sherpa guides that the hair belonged to a yeti. Hillary was evasive when asked about whether he believed such a creature existed: "I am inclined to think that the realm of mythology is where the yeti rightly belongs," Hillary said, although some observers read that quote as a subtle way of saying, *It might exist, and if it does, I hope no one finds it.*

I took another rest break as we climbed the "yetis-have-been-sighted" mountain. I munched a Snickers. I was tired, to be sure, but my modest efforts couldn't compare with the travails of serious yeti-hunters, like my friend Jeffrey McNeely.

During a two-year stint in the mountains of eastern Nepal, conservationist McNeely found yeti spoor at his team's study site between Mount Everest and Mount Kanchenjunga, some two-weeks walk from the nearest road.

The first evidence was a large human-like stool near the camp, which McNeely initially thought came from one of the porters. But the stool included chunks of partly digested bone and hair, perhaps from a serow, a Himalayan antelope.

Then one December morning, McNeely and his colleagues woke to find distinctive footprints in the fresh snow around their tents. "They were about an American size 12 [European size 45] and quite wide. Our first thought was that they might be footprints of a bear," said McNeely, co-author of *Mammals of Thailand*. "But no; these had a round heel while bears have a pointed heel, and there were no claw marks, which would have been present if it had been a bear."

They followed the footprints for a couple hundred meters, until the tracks disappeared into a gulch.

McNeely took some photos and made plaster casts of the footprints. He asked a friend, Andrew Laurie, to carry them out of the country to Bangkok, where McNeely and his colleagues lived.

The casts were carefully packed in an aluminum case, which Laurie, who had been studying Indian rhinos in the Chitwan area of Nepal, carried as hand luggage. At the airport security screening, he was asked what he was carrying, and he explained that they were plaster casts of animals.

"Yeti?" asked the Nepalese customs inspector?

"Er, yes," Laurie replied.

"In that case they're a national treasure," the customs man said, confiscating the case and its contents. They were never seen again.

I asked McNeely what he thought he had discovered.

McNeely is a good friend, whose comments sometimes verge on the cynical. He's a pragmatic scientist who isn't afraid to speculate on what might be. The absence of proof does not mean proof of absence.

"I can't confirm it was a yeti," he said. "But I hold out hope it might be."

I suggested that the never-ending search for the yeti would only be solved one way or another if someone captured an animal.

"You're right," he said, "but I hope it's never found."

"But you believe in the yeti?" As I said it, I realized it sounded like a religious question.

He caught my drift and replied, "The local people certainly believe it." And then my American friend gave a Gallic-type shrug, as if to say, "Who knows?"

The walk to Khramai turned out to be further and harder than I had anticipated. We gained about a thousand meters (3,200 feet) in elevation to reach an altitude of 4,200 meters (14,000 feet). We finally came upon a substantial two-level building, framed by wild rhododendrons beginning to bud. I marveled at the skill of Bhutanese carpenters to build big, sturdy structures in unlikely places. The bottom level was devoid of furniture but dry and moderately clean. The upper floor contained a small chapel, still in use by passing yak-herders. No doubt it would shelter people, and their spirits, through rude winters.

Our home for the night was built about a hundred years ago by a Tibetan monk who lived in the village just below Ogyen Choling.

My night at Khramai passed uneventfully. As I expected we heard no gentle owl-like "hoo-hoo" sounds that would have signaled that a yeti was up and about. I slept peacefully, as did Norsangla. The fire burned until about 10 at night, fragrant with juniper smoke. After that, we were alone with the stars and wind that rippled the prayer flags.

I wasn't disappointed at not having a yeti sighting because I hadn't expected one.

We returned to Ogyen Choling around midday. "Any luck?" Kunzang asked as we shared a quick bite of lunch. I laughed and shook my head.

Kunzang and I then wandered over to the temple to see what my wife was getting up to.

Monique was with Karma, our guide who had just accompanied me on the yeti trek.

"Look what we found!" Monique said. She parted a curtain above a dark doorway. I didn't see anything. "Look with the flashlight," she instructed, and I saw a painting, about 25-centimeters (10-inches) high, of two long-haired, human-like creatures. They formed a couple, and the male had his arm around the female, who had long droopy breasts.

"It's a yeti!" Karma said.

"I grew up here; I've used this temple since I was a little girl, and I never saw this," Kunzang said. She called for her husband.

Walter ran in, thinking someone had been injured. "Look at what Monique and Karma found!" Kunzang said.

Karma's comment was more prosaic. "We didn't have to hike up the mountain to find a yeti. We've got one right here."

SEARCHING FOR SMALL FOLK AT THE END OF THE TRAIL
A Search for Three Types of Hobbits on the Isolated Indonesian Island of Flores

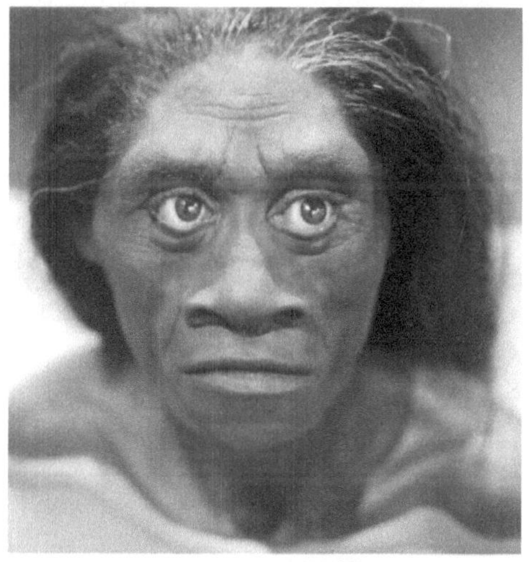

An artist's reconstruction of Flo, a *Homo floresiensis* who lived on Flores island, Indonesia.

FLORES, INDONESIA

Imaginary short people fascinate us, and they take up an inordinate amount of space in literature and mythology. We're all familiar with the Lilliputians who entrapped Gulliver; Snow White's pals Dopey, Sleepy, Grumpy and the rest of the Seven Dwarfs; the Munchkins in the Wizard of Oz; the dwarf Mime in Wagner's Ring cycle; Rumpelstiltskin; and, of course, Tolkien's Hobbits.

Most cultures relish their "short folk" stories. The Irish have their leprechauns, the Icelanders their elves, Hawaiians their menehunes, and Scandinavians their tomtar. Worldwide, people have given at least 200 tongue-caressing appellations to imaginary small folk — *abatwa, bugalademujs*, not to mention *Issun-bōshi, jimaninos* and *jimaninas, naiads*, and *nixies*, and, lest we forget, *pixies, selkies, sluagh, sprites, sylphids, vardogls, wichtlein, yumboes*, and *zips*.

I traveled to the eastern Indonesian island of Flores, some 500 kilometers (320 miles) east of Bali, with my friend Boedhihartono to find *orang pendek*, the Indonesian name for "little people." These small people are the stuff of legends throughout Southeast Asia, and Flores is a rich fishing ground for small-folk tales.

But fables told around the campfire are no substitute for the real thing, and Flores, a dramatically beautiful volcanic island of 1.4 million people that is 2 1/2 times the size of Bali, is home to three items of particular interest to orang pendek researchers.

The first reason to visit Flores is to explore the site of the discovery in 2003 of a prehistoric child-sized creature that scientists declared to be a new species of the genus *Homo*; they named the group *Homo floresiensis*. Researchers said these primates, standing less than a meter tall (about the height of a modern three-year-old American child), with heads the size of grapefruits and weighing just 25 kilograms (55 pounds), lived about 18,000 years ago and were contemporary with *Homo sapiens* but were not direct ancestors of our species. These dates, however, were revised in 2016, with estimates that the new hominin, which scientists informally dubbed Hobbit, was 50,000 to 60,000 years old. Different bones and teeth representing as many as 12 *Homo floresiensis* individuals have been recovered at Liang Bua (Cold Cave) in western Flores — the only site where *Homo floresiensis* has been found so far.

The second trigger for visiting Flores was to investigate tales of *ebu gogo*, an orang pendek-like creature that inhabits the folk tales, if not the contemporary forests, of contemporary Flores.

The third, and most compelling reason was a statement that Boedhihartono had made a few months earlier, in which he had confidently declared "there are *real* Hobbits living in a village in Flores." To which the only appropriate response was: "Are you free in July?"

———◆———

Orang pendek-like creatures in Asia are so frequently mentioned in folk tales and anthropological literature — *tua yeua* in Thailand, *ye ren* of China, *batutut* of Sabah, *sedapa* of Sumatra, *uyan* of Sarawak, and *nguoi rung* of Vietnam — that in our book *Soul of the Tiger*, Jeff McNeely and I dubbed them Untrahom (Unidentified Tropical Asian Hominoids), or, more colloquially, "snowmen of the jungle."

Reports of wild orang pendek, smaller tropical relatives of the more famous *yeti* or Bigfoot, have occurred frequently enough in China, Indochina, Peninsular Malaysia, Borneo, and Sumatra to merit a skeptical inquiry. Although from a much different geographical region, the tropical Southeast Asian orang pendek occupy a similar cultural niche in tropical Southeast Asia to the Himalayan yeti.

In one frequently quoted sighting, an Indonesian "short person of the forest" was reported on the island of Sumatra during the 1920s. A Dutch settler named van Herwaarden, who found an orang pendek in the deep forest, was quoted by the Belgian naturalist Bernard Heuvelmans:

> "The very dark hair on its head fell almost to the waist … (its) brown face was almost hairless. The eyes were very lively, and like human eyes. The nose was broad with fairly large nostrils, but in no way clumsy. Its lips were quite ordinary. Its canines showed clearly from time to time, they were more developed than a man's. I was able to see its right ear which was exactly like a little human ear."

Some respected scientists give cautious credence to the possibility that orang pendek might exist. John MacKinnon, the only scientist to have studied the three great apes in the wild, said he had found footprints in Sabah, Malaysia, of an unidentified primate that were "so like a man's yet definitely not a man's that my skin crept, and I felt a strange desire to return home."

Human-like apes roam the territory of primal myth. Most of us sophisticated city-dwellers have separated ourselves from these remnants of the collective unconscious. But among Asia's forest people, who are in daily contact with "wild nature," the various forms of ape-men are an ever-present reminder of what it means to be man-like, yet not quite human. The creatures of the twilight world live in the forest, away from people, and people fear and respect both them and their forest home.

Even far from the rainforest, most societies tell tales of ape-men, perhaps because we need to be reminded of what our life might be like if we did not have culture, that uniquely human attribute. As the British philosopher Angus Hall suggests: "We need creatures like these to inhabit that strange borderland between fact and fantasy, and our interest lies not so much in whether they really exist but in the possibility that they may exist."

The most important prehistoric archeological site in Indonesia today is Liang Bua (Cold Cave), where *Homo floresiensis* was discovered. The cave lies 14 kilometers (nine miles) north of the Flores town of Ruteng.

Hendrikus Bandar, the "key keeper" of the cave, showed Boedhihartono and me around.

The cave itself is in the form of a fat crescent, maybe 50 meters (165 feet) across, with several levels opening to a green valley. It was almost too perfect; I could see the site being used as the setting for a cave man movie.

In his book, *A New Human*, Mike Morwood writes that as he was leaving Indonesia after a session of 10 weeks of excavation at Liang Bua, he jokingly asked his colleague Emanuel Wahyu Saptomo, "When are you going to find us a pre-modern hominid skull?" to go with the bones of pygmy elephants, giant rats, and stone artifacts that had been excavated.

His colleagues obliged. Rokus Due Awe, a paleoanthropologist from Flores, describes the eureka moment when they realized they were dealing with something special.

Digging at a depth of some six meters (20 feet), Pak Benny, one of the researchers, found a "whitish expression in the clay," according to Rokus. In his zeal to see more, Benny accidentally sliced off what turned out to be the left brow ridge of the skull of the first *Homo floresiensis* discovered.

Pak Benny fortunately stopped his trowel-work and called Emanuel Wahyu Saptomo to have a look. Wahyu himself wasn't sure what they had discovered and asked Rokus to have a look.

"It's a skull," Rokus said.

"Monkey or human?" Wahyu asked the older man.

"Human," Rokus answered.

"Really? Are you one hundred percent sure?"

"Two hundred percent."

The skull was very soft, "the consistency of wet blotting paper," according to Rokus. They cut around it and took the block of stone back to the Hotel Sindha.

Room 19 of the Hotel Sindha in Ruteng hardly looks like the control center for a mega-scientific discovery. It's spacious enough, at about 16 square meters (172 square feet), and the price is right — $10 a night. The room comes with a plain wooden desk, two twin beds with worn floral linen, cream-colored painted cement walls, a mirror and a pair of electrical wires hanging from the ceiling. In the bathroom, the bright yellow sink has stains that defy analysis. There's no hot water, but the friendly staff will boil up a bucket of water that you can mix with the cold to take a simple bath, which is welcome since Ruteng is at an altitude of 1,100 meters (3,600 feet) and it gets chilly at night.

Before they could study the fossil, the Ruteng crew had to harden the bone, which they did by buying acetone in the local drugstore, which they mixed with epoxy glue. The piece of the skull, of a female who was later named Flo, took three days to dry.

Rokus explains those exciting early days. "First I thought it was from a child about ten-years-old, but after cleaning it, we could see that the teeth were very worn, indicating an age of perhaps 28-30 [equivalent to an age today of 50-60]."

The team had just made one of the most sensational discoveries in the history of paleontology.

Much debate ensued about whether the bones of Flo were evidence of a new species. Mike Morwood, the Australian scientist who was a leader of the research team that excavated the site and published the first scientific papers on *Homo floresiensis*, was convinced, based on the jaw structure, lack of chin, brain capacity, height, relative length of arms and legs, and other details, that they had found a new species. Some scientists, notably Indonesia's Teuku Jacob of Gadjah Mada University, suggest that the individuals found were *Homo sapiens* suffering from microcephaly, a development disorder that causes the head and brain to be much smaller than average. Another theory had been proposed that the individuals were *Homo sapiens* born without a functioning thyroid due to an iron deficiency in pregnancy, which led to severe dwarfism and reduced brain size.

People in this part of Flores tell stories about a local bogeyman, the ebu gogo.

Rokus Due Awe, the scientist who was instrumental in identifying Flo as a hominin, is a Flores native. He remembers that his father warned his children not to leave the house when it was raining, lest they be captured by such a monster. He explained that children were told that the animal ran very fast, was hairy over its entire body, lived in the jungle, stole vegetables from farms, and was smaller than one-meter-tall. I asked Rokus whether he really believed the stories. "Yes," he replied, he did. But, perhaps realizing that he had a persona as a scientist to portray, he added "of course we can't prove anything unless we catch one."

Ground zero for ebu gogo is the region around Ebu Lobo (All Ancestors) volcano, at 2,149 meters (7,000 feet), a prominent landmark. And the main storyteller about ebu gogo, which roughly means "ancestor which eats anything," is Pak Epe, the Kampong Boawae headman who describes a creature with a hairy body that lives in caves, eats raw meat, and climbs vertical rock faces like a lizard. In line with other female ogres found throughout Asia, a female ebu gogo has breasts so pendulous that she can flip them over her shoulder.

Pak Epe tells a campfire legend he has down pat. He's clearly told it numerous times and is particularly keen to show us a business card from a producer of the American TV show *60 Minutes* who interviewed him several years ago.

Pak Epe estimates he's about 69. He's bald on top, with white flyaway hair on the sides. He has sparkling eyes and speaks in clear Indonesian.

His story, which he claims is "thousands of years old," is simple and unsatisfying. Once upon a time, a group of ebu gogo came into a village to steal vegetables from the gardens. For reasons that were not clear, one time they stole a five-year-old boy, who was raised by the ebu gogo. Years later, they sent the wild child back to the village to steal fire (shades of Prometheus), and he was caught. The villagers forced the boy to show them the cave where the ebu gogo lived and the humans proceeded to set fires, which killed all but two of the wild men, who escaped to do something, somewhere.

Boedhihartono and I agreed that, as origin legends go, this is pretty feeble stuff. No mythical elements, nothing mystical or sacred, just an old-wives tale that would probably sound better when told around a campfire with the rice wine flowing. As we leave Pak Epe requests a gift for his time.

We give him a few dollars and ask one last question: "Do the ebu gogo still exist?"

"Probably not," he reluctantly decides.

⚬────◆────⚬

There are many conditions and diseases that can cause short stature, according to Little People of America, a nonprofit organization that provides support and information to people of short stature and their families. By far the most frequently diagnosed cause is achondroplasia, a genetic condition that results in disproportionately short arms and legs; the average height of adults with achondroplasia is 152 centimeters (five feet). The website dwarfism.org says that this condition occurs in all races, with equal frequency in males and females, and affects about 1 in every 40,000 children.

Local people are proud of Liang Bua, and government tourism officials in the regional capital Ruteng are hoping that the *Homo floresiensis* nicknamed "Flo" will do for western Flores what Brigitte Bardot did for St. Tropez. The Ruteng visitors' office has published leaflets and posters showing a rather fanciful drawing of "Flo," and there are plans to pave the dirt road leading to the cave. There are also plans to construct a visitors' center near the cave, but, according to Ardi Suardi, an economics professor at Komodo University in Ruteng, the local villagers who own this land are asking about US $11,000 for property that might be worth a fraction of that amount; negotiations continue.

After wandering around Liang Bua, we visited neighboring Kampong Rampasasa, just a ten-minute walk, to ask what they knew about orang pendek.

We were greeted warmly, as is the case in most Indonesian villages, and escorted into the headman's house, a large airless room with a packed earth floor, half the size of a tennis court, which doubles as the community meeting hall. The headman asked if we would like a welcome ceremony, which came in two sizes: the Traditional Lite for $5, and Traditional with Rice Wine for $10. I remembered Boedhihartono's warning in Jakarta to "be careful what you eat or drink in the villages." In the safe environs of Jakarta, I had asked what he meant, and he vaguely indicated the possibility of magic and spells.

But I happen to think that spells only work if the spellee believes that they work, and figuring we would get better answers for the extra $5, or at the very least contribute a bit to the local economy, we sat and drank, surrounded by the usual assortment of children, old women, and men who hadn't gone to the farms that day.

We were asked to introduce ourselves, and Boedhihartono did the honors. In spite of the glowing words, which made me sound like the inventor of the internet, author of more books than Earle Stanley Garner, and educator of malleable minds the world over, I noticed a wizened old lady look at me with what seemed to be amused skepticism. She murmured, to no one in particular, the universal aspersion used to describe uninvited, inappropriately attired visitors with more money than tact: "*Turis.*"

Regardless, Boedhihartono had me trumped. He was a medical doctor, and after a few swigs of rice wine poured from a large white plastic jerry can, he was swarmed with villagers telling them about their ailments.

Then we asked the requisite questions about orang pendeks. Have they heard any stories? Are they themselves descendants of the folks in Liang Bua? Are any small folks still alive?

And our $10 paid off, or at least confirmed free information we had received earlier. "Not here, but there are some short people up in Kampong Arkel."

So, we set off up the hill.

<hr>

Setting off up the hill is a common experience in Indonesia when searching for strange happenstances. In Sumatra, near Kerinci Seblat National Park, I was looking for tiger magicians who could capture man-eating tigers by singing them lullabies. When I asked educated people living in the large cities of Java and Sumatra about these *pawang harimau*, the answer was usually "we've heard about these things, but that's the domain of our wild, savage, near-naked cousins who live in the snake-infested jungles. Why do you want to go there anyway? No Starbucks in the jungle."

This is the common arrogance of the lowland elite, seen

throughout Southeast Asia. Without saying it, people say: "We're educated, we have a big powerful religion, our centuries-old culture is refined through centuries of subtle evolution, we have good personal hygiene, we have electricity (TV!) and wear attractive clothes and speak several languages, and we don't want to know anything about what our rural forefathers were doing just a few generations ago."

So, I set out to seek tiger magicians, just as I've set out to seek a tribe of giant white cannibals in Halmahera in eastern Indonesia and men in west Java who can turn themselves into thieving pigs. Each time I fly into a provincial capital, people will roughly point in the direction of the mountains. I'll get to the mountains, where the villages become simpler, where there are fewer purchased goods, where there might not be electricity or plumbing, and the people will say: "It's not us, Uncle; you want those crazy dudes across the valley and high up the next ridge. Be careful, they've got magic." So I keep on climbing the increasingly narrow trail, and at the end of the line, far from the nearest road and out of cell phone range, I reach a small village and find people who are quite normal. They have families, they farm, they respect whatever spirits they think are important, they laugh, they cry. And, once in a while, if I ask the right questions in the right way, and if I'm smart enough to figure out "what did that guy *really* say?" I learn some insights.

In a sense, the "over the next hill" attitude reflects the existence of orang pendek stories. By common understanding, people on the coast are handsome, smart, and sophisticated. People in the outback are hillbillies. When you're at the bottom of the social totem pole, how do you maintain your humanity? We define ourselves partly by what we are not. And these end-of-the-line folks have no other social groups to look down on, so they create an intermediate creature that is more-than-ape but less-than-human which confirms their human superiority. These stories consolidate the value and integrity of rural folk, as well as helping to maintain some social control.

From Kampong Rampasasa, we walked half an hour toward Kampong Arkel, then hitched a ride the rest of the way on a passenger truck to reach the top of the steep hill.

Arkel is a small, poor village, without the impressive carvings, statuary, weaving, and visible cultural richness found in some other Flores communities. It has no school. No running water. Sort of the end of the line.

In small villages like Arkel the arrival of any strangers is reason to gather and gawk. The "Hobbits" were waiting for us, almost on cue.

We were quickly introduced to four small people, none of whom was taller than 130 centimeters (four feet three inches). They were the living Hobbits we had sought, the holy grail of our search. It was all too easy.

Four members of the clan's short family were on hand to greet us: Margaretha Ndindis, Petrus Bambut, Yohanes Jerahi, and Laurensius Jema. Other family members were living in different parts of Indonesia, they explained.

Petrus, the patriarch, said he might be 100 years old. Boedhihartono asked him what he did during the "Japanese war," referring to World War II. Petrus said that when the war started, he had just gotten married but had not had children, which would make him about 20 in 1940 and about 85 when Boedhihartono and I visited in 2005. Not 100 as he claimed, but a significant age in any case.

Laurensius Jema is *kepala adat* of the village, the keeper of the traditions. He's married to a woman of normal height and has four children; his brother Yohanes has five children.

Their aunt, Margaretha Ndindis, was also of an advanced age, and she asked Boedhihartono for medicine to treat a chronic headache. He obliged, giving her a jab of analgesic on her bum, watched by curious villagers. His medical advice reflected his own personal health regime — eat lots of pork and drink tea without sugar.

While Margaretha was lying on the mat, Boedhihartono got out his caliper and measured the width and breadth of her skull, her nose length, the width of her mandible and jaw. He might have asked permission to take cranial measurements of the other three small folks, but I don't remember hearing much polite discourse as Boedhihartono also measured Laurensius, Yohanes, and Petrus.

It was getting late, and we had to decide whether to leave immediately to return to Ruteng or stay the night.

I was prepared to stay. I had some energy bars, my hammock, and a nearly full water bottle. I also argued that we had come all this way, and these were the only Hobbits we were ever going to meet so what's the rush.

But for reasons that were logical but ultimately unsatisfying, we left Arkel late that afternoon. Boedhihartono argued that the village people were poor and would be embarrassed because they couldn't feed us. Also, there was no water and no toilet. And he speculated that they were getting bored by us, and we had already asked all our questions and wouldn't get any more information. The unspoken sub-text was that Boedhihartono was tired and had a cough and wanted to sleep in a bed in town.

On our last day in Flores, an even more intriguing story emerged, again originating from the isolated northern coast of the island.

Hearing of our interest in strange creatures, we were approached by a gentleman named Pak Nico, who said that in his isolated coastal village one night he heard a screeching cry. It "sounded like something out of that dinosaur movie," he said, referring to *Jurassic Park*, which apparently had made its way to the TV broadcasts of this distant corner of Indonesia. He did not see anything, but his fellow villagers swore they had viewed a frightening T-Rex-like creature that climbed trees and ate pigs and goats. It's called *marengket* in the local Mangarai language, Pak Nico said. Boedhihartono and I were still skeptical, since tales of orang pendeks and their ilk are frequent, and until you capture one, you ain't got nothin'. But Pak Nico added that several years ago, a villager had killed one of the marenkets but had neglected to keep the bones. Imagine, a relict dinosaur that lives on the north coast of Flores. And I know where it is — a long day's journey in a four-wheel-drive vehicle, then a couple of hours walk. Not far at all …

In Search of...

THE MANIPULATED INNOCENTS, THE UNHERALDED HEROES

"Lost" Indonesian Jews Recruited to Fulfill Biblical Prophecy
Small Clan Taken to Israel to Hasten Second Coming

Paul Spencer Sochaczewski

Paulus Mauky at his uncle Hermanus Mauky's grave. The tombstone, donated by Rumondang M. Sitompul, features a Christian cross but no Jewish symbols. The English version of the Indonesian inscription, from Deuteronomy 32:10: "In a desert land he found him, in a barren and howling waste. He shielded him and cared for him; he guarded him as the apple of his eye."

KISAR ISLAND, MALUKU ISLANDS, INDONESIA

This is a story of serendipity and remarkable zeal born of one woman's lifetime religious quest. It is a tale of unasked for fame for simple people and of journeys they had never imagined. All because a determined woman from a distant tribe received a sign from God and suddenly appeared in the orbit of a few unassuming villagers.

The main players in this faraway adventure:

- Herlewen Hermanus Mauky, the elder of a clan living on the tiny and isolated eastern Indonesian island of Kisar. Mr. Hermanus, who died in 2012 at the age of 93, was referred to on this predominantly Christian island as "Hermanus the Jew." Mr. Hermanus, curiously, never claimed to be Jewish.
- Paulus Mauky, Herlewen Hermanus Mauky's nephew, a humble man upon whom the mantle of "the Kisar Jew" has been bestowed.
- Rumondang M. Sitompul, a woman on a mission. She is an evangelical Christian from the western Indonesian island of Sumatra, a distance from Kisar similar to that of Los Angeles to Miami. She has made it her life's work to fulfill biblical prophecy by locating the world's "lost" Jews and transporting them to Israel to hasten the Second Coming of Christ.

⋯⋯⋯⋯◇⋯⋯⋯⋯

I got interested in the Jews of Kisar from reading a few lines in *Indonesia, Etc.*, a book by journalist Elizabeth Pisani in which she mentioned meeting a man in Kisar named Hermanus, who "is said to belong to the Lost Tribes of Israel." She wrote Hermanus was whisked off to the Holy Land by "a busybody Christian from Jakarta to hasten the Second Coming of Christ."

This seemed like a suitable quest, one that involved arduous travel and little likelihood of success. The only certainty was that I'd probably get a dinner-party anecdote out of the trip. All told, plenty of reasons to go.

⋯⋯⋯⋯◇⋯⋯⋯⋯

Kisar island was previously accessible only by boat. Now Susi Air (a private airline owned by Susi Pudjiastuti, the popular Indonesian minister of Maritime Affairs and Fisheries) flies from larger airports to Kisar several times a week, an example of the dramatic improvement in domestic transportation options making life easier for people living on many of Indonesia's vast archipelago.

My friend Boetje Balthazar, a native of Kisar who lives in Jakarta and works in the oil and natural gas industry, and I took motorcycle taxis to the simple home of Paulus Mauky, the senior member of the Clan of Lost Jews.

Paulus, 52, was open and welcoming. His home is simple — cement floor, unpainted plaster walls with a few family photos hanging on nails, and faded curtains in doorways. He has curly gray-black hair and smiles easily. The grave of his uncle Hermanus, who died in 2012, sits prominently in his front yard. Next to the grave stands a waist-high concrete platform. The stones cemented on top represent the tribes of Israel, Paulus says. "It used to have a menorah sitting on top, but the kids broke it."

Years earlier, Ibu Ondang, as Rumondang M Sitompul is known, convinced Hermanus, Paulus, and two other relatives that it was their obligation as Jews to travel with her to Israel. She explained such a journey would help her achieve her life mission — searching the world for "lost" Jews and bringing them to the Holy Land to fulfill the biblical prophecy that the Second Coming of Jesus (and the subsequent Rapture) can take place only after all Jews have gathered in Israel.

We talk about Paulus's trip to Israel, his excitement and trepidation about flying, the buzz of visiting strange countries, and his biggest apprehension of all — *what have I gotten myself into?* He returned from the Holy Land with a few souvenirs. Ibu Ondang sent him a CD with 3,000 photos of the trip, but it's misplaced somewhere in the house. No matter, he doesn't own a computer and has no way to view the pictures. He has Ibu Ondang's phone number somewhere, but again it doesn't matter, since he has no cell phone.

I sense Paulus is a bit overwhelmed by the attention, perhaps unsure of my motives. For a start, I'm a foreigner, and foreigners are rare visitors. I am accompanied by Boetje, a respected elder of Kisar, which means that I have symbiotic stature. I take copious notes, scribbling in a school exercise book with Batman on the cover, certainly curious behavior.

A few hundred meters away he shows us the construction that

locals call the synagogue.

It's a spotless new bamboo structure, paid for by Ibu Ondang, who has furnished it with a shofar (a traditional Jewish ram's horn bugle) and colorful banners featuring Old Testament quotations. A bright golden menorah stands in front. Ibu Ondang later told me she has purchased a much larger menorah for the site, some seven-meters (23 feet) tall, which is languishing in the shipping company's warehouse in Kupang, hundreds of kilometers distant, awaiting delivery instructions.

The "synagogue" has never hosted a Jewish religious service. A local evangelical preacher uses it for weekly services of the Bethel evangelical congregation, which Paulus sometimes attends.

I admire Ibu Ondang's boundless energy to scour the world for "lost" Jews. While some people pursue achievable quests with a clear timeline or definition of success — graduate university, write a book, make puff pastry, visit Rome, taste civet coffee — Ibu Ondang's quest is unlikely to be completed during her time on Earth. But she's engaged in an all-consuming journey that she believes will reward her at some unimaginable time in the future.

I met Ibu Ondang in downtown Jakarta at a modern café next to a movie theatre in an upscale shopping mall. She wore an elegant, black, folk-patterned dress with a stylish gray turban that could have reflected Islamic, Christian, Jewish, or even Hollywood antecedents. She wore a gold necklace featuring the propitious Hebrew word chai (חי), which means "alive" or "living"; it is the root word of the well-known toast *l'chayim*, "to life." She was accompanied by her daughter, son, and a family friend.

Ibu Ondang seems to have a regular stream of visions that shape her life and have guided her in developing her evangelical church — the Bethesda House of Prayer.

Her ongoing vision is to "search for lost Jewish tribes and ask them to come out." This quest, which started two decades before my visit, has taken her to China, Japan, South Africa, India, Madagascar, Myanmar (Burma), the United States, Poland, Russia, Ukraine, and to the far corners of her native country of Indonesia. Ibu Ondang, is independently wealthy and uses her own funds for this "special calling." In pursuit of her goal, she estimates she has visited some 80 countries and has made the pilgrimage to Israel 80 times.

Her Kisar Vision, as I'll call it, began one night as Ibu Ondang was flying in a chartered plane between the Indonesian part of the island of New Guinea and her home in distant Jakarta. "I looked out the window and saw a huge flame, like a searchlight, coming from a tiny island far below," she said. On her return to Jakarta, she asked her son to try to identify the source of the light. "Timor," he said, referring to a huge island about the size of Sicily. "No, it was a tiny island," she said. Finally, based on input from Ibu Ondang and the pilot, her son triangulated the location as Kisar island, which sits to the north of the eastern tip of Timor-Leste. It is four times closer to Australia than to the Indonesian capital of Jakarta.

Not one to prevaricate, Ibu Ondang flew to Kisar. She arrived at Kisar's airstrip (the clean and functional airport building is about as big as a suburban living room) with no advance planning other than a dream that she was destined to visit a sacred site and meet spiritual people. She looked around for transportation. The arrival of a small aircraft at Kisar usually results in a couple of motorcycle taxis and maybe a public van available to carry passengers to their destinations. In this instance, a lone car, one of the few on the island, was waiting.

"The driver asked me where I wanted to go," Ibu Ondang recalled, as we enjoyed espresso and pastries. "I told him I had no idea, only that I had a vision that a holy man would be waiting for me."

"Oh, that would be Hermanus the Jew," the man replied.

The driver was Yohanis Tahinlaru, also a member of the Jewish clan.

And like in a Hollywood movie, when they arrived at his village, Hermanus was waiting in front of his house to receive Ibu Ondang.

"He hugged me and cried. He was very emotional," she told me, "like he had been waiting a long time for my arrival."

One potential stumbling block was that Hermanus didn't identify as a Jew. "He didn't have a religion but told me he believed in a higher power," Ibu Ondang said. "We didn't have a common language but communicated through a spiritual language."

Hermanus took Ibu Ondang to sacred places on Kisar that few outsiders are allowed to visit. On one holy hill, she blew the shofar she had brought with her. "This is a confirmation from the Bible, this is someone sent by our heavenly father," Ibu Ondang recalls Hermanus saying.

Ibu Ondang said she wanted to take Hermanus and three other members of his family to Israel. Besides Hermanus, the group included Paulus Mauky, Yohanis Tahinlaru — the serendipitous driver who had met Ibu Ondang at the airport, and another family member, Jery Mauky.

Imagine. Hermanus at the time was around 90 years old. He had never been further than the provincial capital of Ambon. He had never been on a plane. He spoke a local dialect and only a few words of Bahasa Indonesia, the national language. And while he might indeed have been a spiritual man, he never identified as a Jew.

And there was a mundane but serious problem. Neither Hermanus nor his relatives had Indonesian identity cards, and without identify cards, they couldn't get passports. Yet Ibu Ondang managed to weave her way through Indonesian bureaucracy and got the men passports in one month, surely a record, which she accomplished, she says, "with God's help."

There was a final hurdle. The local government official refused to let them go. According to Ibu Ondang, the local authority said, "Hermanus belongs in Kisar, and we're afraid he won't come back." While indeed that might have been her intention, Ibu Ondang promised that she would bring him and the other three Kisar residents back to the island; she established a bank guarantee for that vow.

Although 87 percent of the people of Indonesia identify as Muslim, the country has no state religion. Among the minority religions, some 10 percent of the country identify as Christian; Kisar itself is largely Protestant. Indonesia has no formal diplomatic ties with Israel, and according to a 2017 BBC World Service poll, 64 percent of Indonesians viewed Israel's influence negatively. Nevertheless, the two countries maintain quiet trade, security, and tourism contacts. Indonesian visitors generally enter Israel with a group tour that begins in Jordan or Egypt.

Ibu Ondang took her Kisar pilgrims on a long and tiring journey. Grasping their shiny new dark green passports (embossed on the front with the Garuda, the mythical Hindu golden eagle that is the coat of arms of Indonesia), they flew to the city of Kupang. Then to Jakarta. Then to Singapore. And on to Jordan.

During the trip, the miracles and visions continued. According to Mrs. Ondang:

- The first time Hermanus set foot in Jerusalem, the earth shook.
- At the grave of Abraham and Sarah in Hebron, Hermanus wept uncontrollably. When he touched the wall of the tomb, the vibration was so strong that Ibu Ondang felt it from several meters away.
- Holy men made a special effort to meet him.
- Local officials said he must stay in Israel.
- Hermanus confessed his sins and asked to be baptized — in the "real" Jordan river, "not the tourist place." When he was baptized, they noticed three beautiful birds that had not been seen before.

So, are Hermanus and Paulus and the others in their clans Jews? And if so, how did their ancestors wind up in Indonesia?

Ibu Ondang says they are remnants of the Tribe of Gad, one of the Lost Tribes of Israel.

Hermanus is said to have speculated that a large fleet of ships from either India or China sailed through Indonesian waters centuries ago and deposited a Jewish man and woman at each place they stopped.

Another, more likely theory, is that during various visits in centuries past a few Portuguese and Dutch merchants and soldiers of Jewish descent settled in Kisar (and other parts of Indonesia), married local women, and started a now-barely visible lineage of Jews, a fraction of the estimated 20,000 descendants of Jews still living in Indonesia. Ayala Klemperer-Markman, author of *The Jewish Community of Indonesia*, notes that "the history of the Jews in Indonesia began with the arrival of early European explorers and settlers, and the first Jews arrived in the 17th century. Most of Indonesian Jews arrived from the Netherlands, Middle East, Northern Africa, and Southern Europe. [Practicing] Jews in Indonesia presently form a very small Jewish community of about 100-500, of mostly Sephardi Jews." Various sources identify small Jewish communities scattered throughout Indonesia, but none mention the Jews of Kisar.

Paulus doesn't know whether he is Jewish. He has no idea about his family's history. Other people I spoke with on Kisar are similarly vague about the origin of these Lost Jews.

Perhaps they are simply crypto-Jews, misidentified people given a new, tenuous backstory.

To Ibu Ondang such questions are irrelevant. "This is not about the religion of Judaism but about the descendants of Israel."

Kisar's Effort to Achieve Global Religious Fame

Paul Spencer Sochaczewski

Boetje Balthazar had a dream and convinced the mayor of Kisar
to turn the small, isolated Indonesian island into a sacred site of
global importance. They envisioned building a World Spiritual
Tourism City to which the righteous of all faiths would flock.
To date, the only constructions are Christian, as reflected by the
crosses in the island's Meditation Garden.

In 2009, Jacob "Jopy" Patty, the regent of Kisar, made an ambitious announcement: Kisar would become a World Spiritual Tourism City. "The island is like Israel," he explained, noting that both territories are green and seasonally lush while their neighboring territories are brown and barren. Both Kisar and Israel have sites sacred to major religions. Both Kisar and Israel have a reputation for magic and miracles. The people of both nations drink wine in festivals and have strong cultures. People of both lands believe that regardless of where you die your body has to be buried in the place of your birth. And both Kisar and Israel have sheep and goats.

169

He concluded: Build the appropriate monuments, and they will come.

Like many big ideas, this concept was based on a vision, one which was remarkably similar to that of Ibu Ondang's.

One night in his home in Jakarta, Boetje Balthazar dreamed that he was on a ship sailing from Timor to Kisar. He saw a large cross on a hill and asked the ship's crew for the name of that place. When he awoke, Boetje called Jacob Patty, and both agreed it was an important confirmation that Kisar is a sacred site of global importance and that the righteous of the world should be invited to visit.

But what would these global pilgrims come to see? What would be a suitable object to attract religious tourists?

The answer, Jopy Patty decided, was a cross. A prominent cross.

I visited the first of Mr. Patty's constructions. On a scenic hill looking across to Timor-Leste, civic authorities, aided by local church volunteers, erected a three-meter-tall (10 foot) wooden cross. That cross has since been neglected and has crumbled into pieces. Even in its heyday, I doubt it had the crowd appeal of, say, the Christ the Redeemer statue in Rio de Janeiro.

A few hundred meters away, on an adjacent hill, a second, more ambitious, memorial was built. Called Taman Meditasi (Meditation Garden), three three-meter-tall, white-painted crosses perch near the summit. The view is magnificent, the space is reasonably well-maintained (a few garbage receptacles would be useful), but it is rarely visited and determinedly mono-religious, hardly the ecumenical pilgrimage destination envisaged by Jacob "Jopy" Patty.

"Look Here, Sir, What a Curious Bird"

What I Learned about Quests by Writing an "Enhanced Biography" of a Little-Known 19th-Century Teenager from Borneo

Trustees of the Natural History Museum, London

Hand-colored lithograph of Semioptera walacii by John and Elizabeth Gould from John Gould's The Birds of Australia. *Trustees of the Natural History Museum, London*

Ali, and the bird of paradise he shot, now named after Alfred Russel Wallace. Ali greatly helped Wallace on his adventures. I suggest each of us also owes a big thanks to people like Ali who have assisted on our quests and journeys, perhaps without receiving sufficient recognition.

For more than 50 years I've been following the trail of Alfred Russel Wallace, one of history's greatest naturalists, thinkers, and social commentators.

Wallace was assisted by a young man named, simply, Ali. Without Ali, Wallace would not have been as successful as he was.

171

This is the story of the search for Ali, in particular the quest to learn Ali's family name, determine his background, and to speculate on what he thought about traveling with a remarkable, and probably seemingly quite odd, Englishman.

In a way it's also the story of all our lives. Has there been someone who has quietly aided you in your quests but hasn't received adequate recognition or thanks?

To summarize Wallace's eventful and productive life:

Wallace was born in 1823, in Wales just across the border from England. He left school at the age of 14 and became interested in natural history, particularly beetles. In 1844, curious about the biology of distant lands, and getting restless in the UK, he and his friend Henry Walter Bates said to each other: *Hey, let's go to the Amazon.*

Consider the boyhood-bravado of that intention. Wallace, 25, and Bates 23, had never left England. They had no independent income and gambled that the wildlife specimens they collected would earn them enough money to survive. They had no formal training in biology, taxonomy, or collecting. Unlike other Victorian explorers, the two young men had no government mandates, no military backup, no diplomatic status, no academic credentials, and no important people ready to bail them out in the event of trouble. And neither spoke Portuguese.

Wallace's four years on the Amazon and Rio Negro ended disastrously, when the brig *Helen*, on which he was returning to England, caught fire. Wallace spent 10 days in a lifeboat before being rescued; he lost virtually his entire collection and almost his life. He swore never to get on another boat.

But he did. He received a grant from the Royal Geographical Society to explore the Malay Archipelago, a region that includes today's Singapore, Indonesia, Malaysia, and Timor-Leste.

His remarkable haul included 125,660 individual specimens, including 900 *new* species of beetles, 50 *new* species of butterflies, 212 *new* species of birds, and, incredibly, 200 *new* species of ants. He also independently developed the Theory of Evolution by Natural Selection.

And he did this without a support system or a guaranteed income or trust fund.

In the eight years he traveled in Asia, Wallace covered more than 22,000 kilometers (14,000 miles) and made some 100 different collecting expeditions, often sailing to tiny, isolated islands. To reach rarely visited destinations, he often had to buy, borrow, or build his own boat, and hire local men for various services. On arrival he had to ask the local headman for permission to build a shelter in the forest. He suffered debilitating fevers, a multitude of injuries, deprivations, and, we might imagine, loneliness. When it rained, he and his collection got soaked. He had to fend off scavenging ants, rats, and dogs who wanted to eat his specimens. He had to try to identify what he had collected (and wrote several times of the joy of finding a new species) while preparing the shipment for the long voyage back to London.

Contrast Wallace's experience with that of Charles Darwin. Two decades earlier Darwin sailed around the world on the Beagle, a Royal Navy ship which was, in effect, a floating base camp. He had a safe, dry place to keep his supplies and specimens, military protection under Queen Victoria's flag, and sailors on board who could do his laundry, cook for him, and tend to him when he was seasick, which he was almost every day of the voyage.

Compared to other Victorian-era explorers, Wallace gave robust credit to the men he hired as collectors, carpenters, boatmen, and por-ters, some 1,300 people, by one reckoning. But *primus inter pares* was a 15-year-old Malay lad named Ali, who Wallace hired in 1855 while in Sarawak, then under the rule of James Brooke, the famous White Rajah of Borneo, now a Malaysian state on the island of Borneo. Ali (we don't know his full name) evolved into a reliable camp manager and preparer of bird skins. He was also an expert bird collector, and, by some accounts, was responsible for shooting some 5,000 of the 8,050 bird specimens Wallace collected. Wallace wrote that Ali was his "head man" and "faithful companion," and we can safely speculate that Wallace would not have been as successful as he was without Ali's support.

And here are the suppositions and mysteries, which fascinate me more than the facts:

What did teenage Ali think of this tall, strange European man who swooned over a new beetle, cuddled a baby orangutan he had orphaned, and lived rough in the forest? Did Ali giggle each time he heard Wallace speak in strongly accented Malay? If Wallace had asked, would Ali have returned to England with him? What did Wallace teach Ali? What did Ali teach Wallace? Where did Ali go after Wallace left? Can we find Ali's descendants to spur a conservation movement? And, for fun, could I speak with Ali's spirit through a medium? These questions have sparked my interest for some 50 years.

I find writing history a slippery exercise.

Most academic historians study peer-reviewed, multi-footnoted journal articles by respected researchers, dig through dusty letters and chronicles, then evaluate and triangulate until, like Miss Marple, they reach what to them is a convincing solution to a particular puzzle. But a life, and therefore a history of a life, is seldom as neatly binary as Sherlock Holmes might have us believe. Daniel Warner, author of *An Ethic of Responsibility in International Relations*, says: "In writing history there is no absolute 'truth,' only a multitude of lesser lower-case facsimiles we might term 'truths.'"

Most everything we consider as "fact" related to Ali comes from Alfred Russel Wallace's writing. Wallace was a careful writer; for example, he told us how many moths he collected on January 31, 1855, on a Sarawak night that was "dark and windy; heavy rain (200, of 130 species)," the exact dimensions of his house in Ternate ("Hall. 20 x 18"), the detailed descriptions of how to process sago, and the dimensions of the crania of individuals he described as of Malay, Papuan, Polynesian, and Australian ethnicities. Nevertheless, when writing about incidents and emotions, he filtered his story. He selected what he was going to tell us, then edited how to explain his challenges and accomplishments. We can't fault him for this, because we all choose what to remember and how we choose to report it. Similarly, we, the listeners and readers, also process information in unique ways. Can you remember, verbatim, word for word, a conversation you had an hour ago? Can you retell an event you participated in without amplifying, pruning, or enhancing? We live in a world of non-stop Chinese whispers.

With Wallace's extensive writing (some 20 books, 600 articles, and hundreds of letters), we learn quite a bit about the facts of his life. But what about his inner life? What psychological triggers might have catalyzed Wallace's desire to leave England and explore the world? How did he overcome the trauma of losing much of his South American collection, and almost his life, when the ship he was on caught fire and sank? How did he manage to compartmentalize so successfully: In *The Malay Archipelago* he writes about shooting and killing a female orangutan, rescuing the baby she had been nursing, trying to care for the infant, writing sentimental paragraphs about how cute it was, and then, when the baby died, boiling it and selling the skeleton to a museum in England.

———◇———

And what went on in Ali's mind? He was illiterate and left no written record. If he had left us letters or journals, would he have limited himself to the "facts" of his travels with Wallace? Or would he have gone deeper? The six-odd years he spent with Wallace took him places he couldn't have imagined, with experiences that must have stayed with him for life. What was going through his head? What was the trigger to his wanderlust — was it a cultural trait, a personal adventure, or just a way to earn money? Why was he so loyal to Wallace? Did he have ambitions of his own, or was he happy just to go along for the ride? Did he think Wallace was an entitled but silly white man who used perfectly good guns to shoot tiny birds for his collection instead of deer for a barbecue? And what about all those too-tall, too-loud, over-dressed white men whom Wallace called friends, with their impressive technology, huge houses, and seemingly innate ability to read, write, and apparently rule the world? Were they cash cows waiting to be milked? Were they to be respected, admired, or even emulated? Or were they foreign interlopers, temporary irritants in Allah's grand scheme of things?

I don't have answers. I do have speculations and triangulations, a series of jigsaw pieces that seem to make sense. Two adventuring Englishmen of the period (Frederick and Arthur Boyle) refer to a young man named Ali who they hired post-Wallace and who could well be the same Ali who worked with Wallace. And in 1907, respected American naturalist Thomas Barbour met "a wizened old Malay" on Indonesia's Ternate island who identified himself as "Ali Wallace." All tantalizing clues.

We'll probably never know Ali's family name. Maybe it doesn't matter. Maybe we should leave Ali as an interesting footnote in history. But we also might use Ali as a trigger to ask ourselves the question: Is there someone in your life who has quietly helped you, perhaps without adequate recognition, on your journey?

Laos White Elephant Settles in After Long March

Communist Leaders Use the Animal to Co-Opt the Power and Prestige of Buddhist Kings, Depriving Village Farmer His Shot at Glory

Paul Spencer Sochaczewski

Boun Somsy, with a painting of his white elephant that was liberated by the power-hungry wife of the country's first president.

BAN SAMING, LAOS

Capturing a rare white elephant usually brings luck and fame, and it did for Boun Somsy, at least for a while.

Then a couple of wannabe-royals stepped in and rained on his parade.

This is a tale of prophetic (and sensual) dreams and an unexpected windfall. It is also the tale of how an areligious communist government usurped a potent Buddhist religious symbol, and as is so often the case, nature conservation.

<hr>

In December 1983 a poor farmer named Boun Somsy had a dream in which a beautiful woman, "dressed like a god," came to his simple house and told him to "go find a diamond." In his village of elephant hunters, 60 kilometers (37 miles) from the southern Laotian city of Pakse, Boun interpreted her cryptic instructions as telling him to "go catch a white elephant."

The problem was that Boun, then 39, had never caught any elephant, which is a bit like telling a couch potato to go run a marathon.

Nevertheless, Boun instructed his wife to refrain from combing and oiling her hair, which he thought would have made his hunting ropes slippery. The elephant-hunters slept rough in the forest in a simple shelter. On the fifth night of the hunt for the Lao equivalent of the Holy Grail, Boun had another dream. Same beautiful woman, similar message. "I will give you this mansion," she said, gesturing toward her estate. The next morning Boun spotted and captured a juvenile female elephant. Upon bringing the dirty animal back to the village and giving it a good scrub, he saw that it was "the color of old bamboo," a rare and holy white elephant.

Devotees, some from distant villages, came to pay homage to his white elephant, leaving behind offerings and some much-welcomed cash.

News of his special elephant spread, and a Cambodian elephant trader offered him ten "normal" elephants for the white pachyderm. But before Boun could close the deal a government official named Sali knocked on the door of his village house with the Laotian equivalent of "I'm from the government, and I'm here to help you."

Sali and four white elephant adjudicators (surely the most arcane of Asian job descriptions) inspected the animal and gave Boun the good news that he would have the honor of donating the auspicious beast to the citizens of the fledgling People's Republic of Laos. In olden days, the animal would have been offered to the king, but Prince Souvanna Phouma, the nation's top-ranking royal, had been deposed in 1975 as prime minister by communist leader Kaysone Phomvihane, making commoners Kaysone and his wife, Thongvinh Phomvihane, de facto royalty in the social hierarchy.

Boun was instructed to ride the people's elephant to the capital of Vientiane, a journey north that took 29 days.

He was offered no compensation or public gratitude.

Why did Kaysone Phomvihane and his ethnic-Vietnamese wife Thongvinh want the white elephant?

The white elephant is seen as a religious miracle, a descendant of the holy white elephant that Queen Maya dreamed entered her body nine months before Prince Siddhartha, who was to become the Buddha, was born. The white elephant historically represents the power of the Buddhist kings of the region, and the kings of neighboring Burma, Thailand, and Cambodia fought a series of wars between 1549 and 1769 dedicated, in part, to stealing each other's white elephants. Kaysone Phomvihane (whose name derives from a Pali word describing the four sublime states of mind achieved by a Buddhist monk), the first prime minister, and later president of communist Laos, simply wanted to be viewed as a fair, righteous, and powerful king.

Or, more likely, observers suggest, his wife wanted to be viewed as a fair, righteous, and all-powerful queen.

Through a well-placed Laotian friend, I was given a rare interview with semi-reclusive Madame Thongvinh. Her Lao husband, Kaysone Phomvihane, was a leader of the Vietnam-supported Pathet Lao. He was a revolutionary hero, and today his self-satisfied and well-fed portrait appears on the country's currency, and an $8 million museum has been built in his honor. To use an American simile, meeting Madame Thongvinh was like getting an interview with

Martha Washington.

Looking like a frail 70-something woman who had just woken from a nap, she was guarded and reticent. She wore a worn house-dress, and we sat in her comfortable but simple house on the out-skirts of Vientiane. She spoke neither French nor English, and my friend translated. After pleasantries on my part, greeted with stoic silence and the reluctant offering of a glass of water on hers, I asked about her white elephant.

"Why do you want to know?" she grunted, followed by a sail-or-quality belch that threatened to wilt the plastic flowers in her living room, where most of the wall space was consumed by pho-tos of her and her husband during their glory days, alongside one dramatic photo of her white elephant.

I explained my long interest in white elephants and desire to know more about white elephants in Lao culture.

"Why do you want to know?"

I tried another tack: I implied that the white elephant repre-sented powerful leaders and asked whether that was the reason her husband wanted the elephant.

"Where are you from?"

"America."

Her face seemed to freeze.

Her industrial-sized belch seemed even more vigorous.

The only moment of softness came when she explained how she loves animals and how she and her elephant are "soul partners" — when she is ill, the elephant also feels ill, and vice versa. She told of her dreams and her visions of the white elephant flying alongside her plane, protecting her whenever she travels overseas.

I showed her the photo of Boun, the villager who captured her elephant. Madame Thongvinh snorted, said the elephant was sick while she was in Boun's care, and threw the photo back on my pile of papers, as if it was dirty.

Why was she so rude and unhelpful?

Pick a reason: She was tired and grumpy. She was not used to speaking with a foreigner. She doesn't like Americans. She was protective of the white elephant, which she considers "her property." She was afraid I would make fun of the richly symbolic animal. She had lost her power, position, and legacy, and the white elephant was the only symbol she had left of the good old days.

◦——————◦——————◦

We had been given permission by the district authorities to visit her white elephant, and the next morning drove to a nature reserve in Phialat, an hour and a half northwest of Vientiane. En route, my Laotian friend called ahead to arrange lunch and was told that our white elephant viewing privileges had been revoked by Madame Thongvinh.

We went anyway and met one of the vets who oversees the care of the animal.

He confirmed that the animal was indeed the personal property of Madame Thongvinh, and her word in the district was law. No, we couldn't see the elephant. Yes, the animal was healthy. Yes, Madame Thongvinh visits about twice a year; she is the only visitor. Yes, she and the elephant have a special relationship. Yes, she instructs that when the elephant is moved from one part of the buffer zone next to the national park to another it is "camouflaged" with dark paint. No, we couldn't slip into the forest and search for it ourselves.

Laos's other white elephant, a male named Chayamongkhol (King of Elephants), died in 2010 at the Laos Zoo. This makes Madame Thongvinh's white elephant, which she's named Keo (Precious), the country's only such creature and the property of a woman who holds on to the idea that the animal will do for her what it has done for Buddhist rulers for centuries — show that she is a legitimate and semi-divine leader. Perhaps the white elephant can compensate for her indignation at being kicked out of her executive position in the Communist Party for excessive corruption (allegedly smuggling heroin to Vietnam). Perhaps the animal can give a feeble old woman who has been sidelined by the younger generation (few people in Vientiane know or care about her) one last glimmer of self-respect.

181

And Madame Thongvinh's elephant might be the last one for a while. While an aerial photo of a wild white elephant, spotted in 1998 by a helicopter pilot, circulated in Lao conservation circles a few years ago, that animal has not been seen since. And the elephant population in Laos, which describes itself as Lan Xang — Land of a Million Elephants (and which had Airavata, the archetypal white elephant, on its flag during the royalist period of 1952-1975) — continues to crash. The IUCN Red List estimates that there are only some 400 wild elephants left in the country, and the number is decreasing.

And Boun, the man who had a dream and captured the animal?

After his epic elephant march to Vientiane to "donate" the elephant to the prime minister and his wife, Boun returned to his village broke and empty handed. A few years later, another government official came to his home with a gift, the only compensation or thanks he ever received. It is a painting on thin wood, about half as tall as he is, showing Boun's daughter, son-in-law, and granddaughter sitting on the white elephant that he captured through a mystical dream.

How Did White Elephants Become So Powerful?

BuddhaLife　　　　*Paul Spencer Sochaczewski*

The Buddhist kings of Thailand, Burma, Laos, and Cambodia have collected white elephants (and fought wars to steal white elephants belonging to their enemies) for centuries. The monarchs believed that ownership of these sacred and rare animals confirmed that they were just, powerful, and divinely anointed rulers.

Like other key Asian symbols, the long cosmological march of the white elephant has its beginnings in local nature-inspired Indigenous beliefs that were subsequently adopted and adapted by proponents of new religions.

In ancient pre-Hindu, pre-Buddhist times, the white elephant was associated with rain clouds and, like the cobra-inspired *nagas*, was a symbol of life and prosperity. It made sense then for Hindu priests to build on this time-proven perception and incorporate elephants into Hindu mythology. The four-tusked white elephant Airavata, who rose to the surface when the celestial Sea of Milk was churned, was an elephant Adam and begat all the elephants which followed. Just as sun-eagle Garuda became the mount of Hindu god Vishnu, the white elephant became the steed of Indra, the Hindu god of the heavens.

Subsequent Buddhist teachers built on the already deep-rooted Hindu beliefs. Airavata, they argued, had been an incarnate Buddha (bodhisattva). But raising the stakes even higher, they said that a holy white elephant appeared in a dream to Lord Buddha's mother-to-be, Queen Maya. The future Buddha, in his elephant form, held in his silvery trunk a white lotus flower (the symbol of the yoni, female genitalia). The white elephant uttered a long, drawn-out cry, bowed three times, and touched his forehead to the floor. Then he gently struck Maya's right side and entered her womb. The queen reported this extraordinary vision to the court astrologers, who divined that she would bring forth a great king or a great seer. Nine months later, Prince Siddhartha was born, the Buddhist equivalent of a virgin birth. Present at the birth was Indra, a powerful Vedic and Hindu god of thunder and rain, offering his hair as a blessing gift and acknowledging Siddhartha as an avatar of Vishnu.

And the connection with the Buddhist kings who fought wars over white elephant trophies?

One needs only look at the symbolism surrounding the late King Bhumibol Adulyadej of Thailand, the world's longest-serving monarch (and owner of 11 white elephants, arguably the most of any Buddhist king). He was a revered ruler whom many considered to be semi-divine. He was referred to as Rama IX, and the use of the name "Rama" clearly positioned him as an avatar of Vishnu, thereby linking him with both Rama (of Ramayana fame) who was the seventh avatar of Vishnu, and with Buddha, who was Vishnu's ninth avatar. To consolidate the symbolism, King Bhumibol's royal emblem featured Garuda (Krut in Thai), which is Vishnu's mount. When one sees the Thai Krut on a government building, it signifies that it is under the protection and control of the Vishnu-related king, quite literally, "the king/Vishnu is in the building."

So, following the circuitous but pervasive logic of Hindu-Buddhist belief systems, King Bhumibol, as well as former Buddhist kings of Burma, Laos, and Cambodia, encouraged the idea that they were related to the most powerful Hindu gods, who themselves are also closely associated with Buddha. The white elephant, which adorned Thailand's flag from 1855 to 1916, is a symbol of that cosmic power, and in the context of Asian Buddhist power-grabs, the monarch with the most white elephants wins.

Last Great Elephant Hunter Achieves Indochine Glory

He's Notched 298 Pachyderms and a Lucrative Product Endorsement Contract

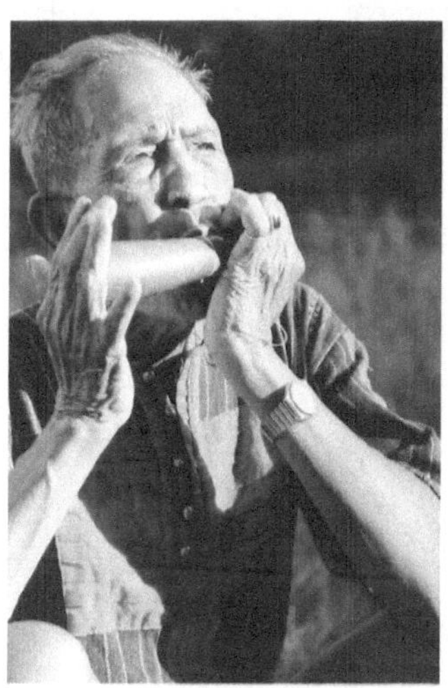

Paul Spencer Sochaczewski

Paul Spencer Sochaczewski

(Left) Ama Kong blowing a horn trumpet that's used to alert
hunters to the presence of wild elephants.
(Right) Ama Kong's signature medicinal wine —
"Good for strengthening a man's back and kidneys"

BUON MA THUOT, CENTRAL HIGHLANDS, VIETNAM

Stardom can be defined in many ways. For Ama Kong it is a number — 298, the sum of wild elephants he has captured. Now 90, with failing eyesight but still with a healthy head of hair, Ama Kong is the Michael Jordan of elephant hunters. By his accounts, he is the second most successful elephant hunter in the country (his late uncle, also named Ama Kong, holds the title, with

487 animals). He proudly shows his elephant-hunter badge of honor — a nasty-looking groin scar inflicted by a wild bull elephant. And Ama Kong has his own signature brand of medicinal wine, the Vietnamese equivalent of having a sneaker named after you. The gold Vietnamese lettering on the wine's striking red box can be translated as: "Good for strengthening a man's back and kidneys," an Asian euphemism indicating that this is a powerful sex tonic.

And Ama Kong is walking proof that his wine works, having sired 21 children from four wives. The tonic might also explain his fine memory, since he is able to remember the names and birthdays of his spouses and offspring, including the youngest, a curious girl of seven named H'Bup Eban, who can't resist clambering onto dad's lap. But there are some things that even herbal tonics can't fix — his upper teeth are bright, intact, and obviously false compared to the red, rotting stumps of his lower teeth, destroyed by years of chewing betel.

The term "hunter" is misleading, since Ama Kong was a "capturer" of wild elephants, never a "killer." His M'Nong ethnic group has long been known for capturing and selling elephants to work in the timber industries. However, he is likely to be the last elephant-hunter superstar — since the animals are protected by Vietnamese law, fewer young people learn the skills today, and most important, there are far fewer elephants around to catch.

Vietnam's elephant population has declined dramatically in recent years, falling to just 114 animals in 2000, down from a maximum estimated population of 2,000 wild animals in 1980.

The domesticated elephant population has similarly declined. In Dak Lak province, where Ama Kong lives, located in the Vietnamese Central Highlands near the Cambodian border, the number of elephants in captivity has decreased to just 138 in 2000 compared to some 300 in 1990.

But how do you capture a wild elephant?

Moving slowly (because even with the help of medicinal wine, at age 90 your arthritis seeps in), Ama Kong demonstrates the procedure.

First, he blows on a trumpet made of buffalo horn to seek the support of the forest spirits. He then explains how he would go into the forest with several domesticated elephants (always an odd number of animals — odd numbers indicate male power; even numbers female power) and look for a herd of wild pachyderms. The domestic elephants are Judas elephants, he explains, since they are able to mingle with the wild herd, even when mahouts sit atop their necks. The group tries to isolate a baby or juvenile ("easier to train than an adult" and a whole lot easier to catch). Using a kind of cowboy-lasso technique, Ama Kong shows how he would entrap the prey's foot with a rattan loop attached to a long stick. The lasso was attached to a hundred-meter-long handmade rope made from water buffalo skin, and as the baby elephant ran, it would get hopelessly entangled in the trees. The domesticated elephants would then take over and escort the kidnapped baby as far as possible from the wild herd. When the elephant hunters camped at night, they lit fires and beat gongs to frighten away the wild elephants that had come to rescue the crying infant.

Ama Kong has also captured eight rare white elephants, which he describes as being "like the French because they have yellow eyes and fair skin." Because of the scarcity of white elephants and their importance in Buddhist cosmology, which in turn consolidates the power of kings, these animals brought him into contact with royalty and political figures, including the kings of Thailand and Laos, Ho Chi Minh, and Emperor Bao Dai of Vietnam.

In 1996, at the age of 86, Ama Kong captured his last elephant. This was five years after his hunting ground was turned into a national park and elephants were declared a protected species.

"It's a shame the government won't let us hunt anymore," he says. "I'm still strong enough to lead a group of hunters into the forest."

THE GIRL BY THE SIDE OF THE ROAD

Twenty-Six Years On, Searching for the Girl Whose Eyes Said, "I'm Going to Surprise You"

Paul Spencer Sochaczewski
Sonam Angmo: "You're looking for my daughter Tsewang?"

LADAKH, INDIA

In 1979 I took a black-and-white photo of a young girl in Ladakh. She was perhaps 10. She wore a rough robe of a red-brown homespun wool, she carried a slate on which she used a stick dipped in muddy water to write her alphabets, and she carried a simple brown-canvas army-style book bag slung over her shoulder.

I have no idea what she was thinking, but to me her gaze said,

189

quietly, "Watch me. I'm going to surprise you."

I sought her out in April 2005.

There was a slight problem, though. I didn't remember where I had taken the photo.

I keep my old journals and found my notes from the trip 26 years earlier. At a town I had identified as Bongzo, I had written about a little girl, whose "hands were rough with ingrained dirt, the texture of sandpaper." We had arithmetic as a common language, and I wrote "2 + 2" and watched her stroke the numeral "4." I gave her a ballpoint pen. "The girl's eyes lit up for a moment with immediate recognition," I had written. "After realizing the pen was for her, she grabbed it, and in one motion, secured it inside her homespun robe."

I was in the remote Himalayan region of Ladakh to write an article about the golf course in Leh, which, at 3,445 meters (11,300 feet), is the world's highest. I had a free day, and understanding my esoteric interests, my guide, Tashi Chotak Lonchey, had taken me to the monastery that I had visited 26 years earlier (one of the monks was still alive, and he recognized himself in a photo). After a cup of butter tea, we decided to drive several hours to visit a sacred forest, an ancient juniper tree grove in Hemis Shukpachan. After driving for about an hour and half, we passed a small village and I saw a sign that said "Basgo." "Maybe this is the place where you took the picture," Tashi suggested. Bongzo? Basgo? Close enough to be worth a detour.

None of it looked familiar. My only thought was that in 1979 my friend David and I must have stopped here for a tea break during a bus ride to a monastery farther along the same road.

The best source of village history is generally an old woman, and at a large house near the road we showed Rigsin Zangchan a blowup of the young girl's photo. "It could be Tsewang," she said after some thought. "Her husband Tashi Angchok is just up the street."

We found Tashi Angchok working at the family restaurant. He offered us tea as he studied the photo. "The smile looks similar to my wife's," he said. But the problem was that his wife, Tsewang Dolma, the reputed girl in the photo, wasn't around since she worked as a teacher at Tridho, a one-class school some three hours away, near the Tibet border.

He took the picture to his mother-in-law, Sonam Angmo, and came back with a handful of old photos showing his wife as a young girl. Sonam said that my photo seemed to be that of her daughter, but she wasn't sure.

We still had a long program ahead of us that day, so we left the photo with Tashi Angchok, told him we would be back at the end of the afternoon, and went to explore the sacred forest in Hemis.

It was almost sundown when we got back to Basgo.

"It's her," Tashi said confidently.

We asked how he knew.

"I showed the picture to Tsewang's sister but didn't say, 'Is this Tsewang?' I simply asked, 'Do you know this girl?'" he said, quite proud of his detective skills. "She said, 'Yes, that's my little sister.'"

So, just like that, I had found a family who invited me to dinner next time I'm in Ladakh. Then I'll get a chance to have a conversation with this girl, now a grown woman, whose photo and spirit has graced my home for a quarter of a century.

⟡

I still haven't met the adult Tsewang Dolma, the cheeky young girl in the photo wearing a *nambu*-style jacket woven by her father. But I've been in regular email contact with her and her sister, who is a Buddhist nun in a nearby temple.

However, I am in close contact with Tsewang's daughter, Dechen Chuskit, and have visited her in Delhi where she was studying philosophy at the prestigious Delhi University. She is now studying for her PhD in Tibetan Buddhist philosophy at a university in Varanasi.

THE ALMOST-LAST SHAMAN
It's Been a Good Ride, but
Borneo Healer Doesn't Expect Many Others
to Follow in His Path

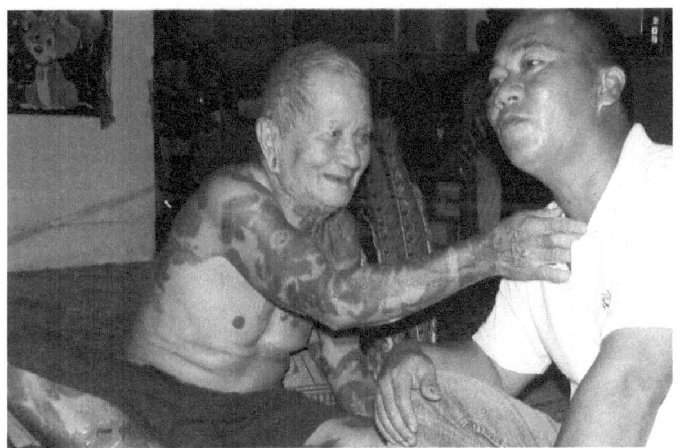

Paul Spencer Sochaczewski

Good bedside manner — Unding anak Libau treats a patient.

SERUBAH ULU, SARAWAK, MALAYSIA

To the untrained eye, he seems an unlikely magician. Frail but with a hundred-watt smile. He has two wispy whiskers and short grey hair, and he walks a bit slowly. But cut him some slack. He's 91, thereabouts. He's got tattoos on his neck, his arms, his legs; not much different from most elderly Iban men. Except unlike most men, Unding anak Libau can chase spirits and make ill people healthy.

Unding anak Libau is a *manang*, a traditional healer, living in a longhouse in Sarawak, not far from the Indonesian border. He's one of the last of his profession.

I first encountered members of the large Iban tribe in 1969 when I

193

was posted to Sarawak, a Malaysian state on the island of Borneo as a US Peace Corps volunteer. Sarawak was changing, quickly. Some people proudly promoted the holy grail of "development" and predicted how improvements in agriculture, economy, education, and health care would improve the lives of the people of the state. I was a naïve 22-year-old, just out of university, and relished my new life travelling in small boats along muddy rivers to visit some-times-shaky wooden longhouses. I advised primary school teachers (who often were much more skilled than I was, sometimes juggling two or three classes in open-air schools) about how to teach more effectively. I trekked in vast swatches of rainforest, admiring glorious hornbills, hunting wild pigs, catching (and dining on) pythons, and bathing in the rivers. I helped slash-and-burn secondary forest so strong-calved men and women could plant hill rice on the steep charred slopes. I drank too much rice wine and made a fool of myself too many times trying to perform local dances. For me, it was a transformative idyl, and I didn't give much thought to Sarawak ever changing. I was far too innocent and idealistic — I didn't spend much time wondering how the Ibans and other indigenous groups would adapt to the benefits and challenges that accompany the inevitable impact of a modern multi-cultural, increasingly well-off, and better-educated, society.

I return to Sarawak every few years, and on one of those visits, I sought advice from three senior Iban academics at the respected Tun Jugah Foundation in Kuching — one objective of which is "To preserve and promote Iban culture, arts and language." Tan Sri Leonard Linggi Jugah, Robert Menua Saleh, and Peter Kedit explained the realities of modern life that threaten the existence of people like Unding. There's the availability of Western education. Fluency in English and Bahasa Malaysia to complement the Iban language. Ease of transport, which means people can easily travel far from their longhouses and mingle with other people and cultures; marriage between Ibans and folks from other ethnic groups is common.

Communications — it's rare (perhaps impossible) to find a longhouse without TV, cell phones, and often internet. Easy access to hospitals and clinics. Enough money to enjoy the consumer economy.

How pervasive are these modern realities in weakening the influence of people like Unding and his Indigenous beliefs?

I conducted an informal, admittedly limited, and totally unscientific survey of young Iban men and women in the state capital of Kuching and the town of Sri Aman, not far from Unding anak Libau's longhouse. I asked them two questions: How many of the major Iban bird omens can you name? And how many players in the English Premier League can you recall?

When given hints, they said they had heard of the bird omens but were hazy about what each one did. They were much more at home discussing English football, and names like Wayne Rooney and Steven Gerrard came without much prompting.

The Iban tribal group are in no danger of disappearing; they comprise some 30 percent of Sarawak's population and are an important political, cultural, and economic force in the state. However, only a handful of manang remain.

Perhaps the main reason why the manang culture is dying is because of that pervasive force of anti-Animism: Christianity.

Religion can be a tricky subject for many families, and it's no different when Unding sits down with his immediate clan. In 1979 Unding's son Galau anak Unding had a dream. He saw two women in white shirts. They saw some ghosts and prayed while holding candles. The ghosts ran away. Galau interprets this as meaning that the two women were Christian, and the Anglican religion can protect people from ghosts.

Galau converted and asked his father to also become Christian. Unding, however, had his own dream, in which Unding's personal spirit guide, the *nyigit* or cicada, appeared and told him that if he became Christian, he would soon be invited to "go join the spirits."

For Unding, this was a clear message that if he converted, he would die. While Unding stayed with the old beliefs, he doesn't mind that a simple dark blue cross is displayed on the front door of his apartment in the longhouse — after all, Christians live within and they're family. Galau, for his part, has become the longhouse's lay preacher.

For the visitor, the Ibans are gregarious and hard-drinking, always ready for a party.

They are also among the most studied tribal groups by anthropologists, who have recorded the Ibans' healing songs, bird omens, courtship rituals (pre-marital sex used to be no big deal), social structure (pretty flat, and women have a strong voice), architecture, weaving, and animal spirit guides — whatever could generate a PhD has been examined and footnoted.

An Iban longhouse resembles a communal single-story motel, where family rooms sit adjacent to each other. Previously made of bamboo and wood (and remarkably photogenic), many longhouses in Sarawak are now made of concrete, with tin roofs. Unding's longhouse, however, is constructed in the traditional style, and the bamboo floors on the common porch bounce a bit when children run past. As you enter, the most striking decoration in the main living room of Unding's family's apartment is a commercially printed poster, about as big as a large bedsheet. It is the kind of canvas banner, printed in town, that middle-class Sarawakians display for birthdays, anniversaries, and business events. It reads *Selamat Ari-Jadi-90* (Happy 90th Birthday) and features a large photo of Unding, a dozen colorful balloons, and prominent images of Tweety Bird and the cute dog Lady (from *Lady and the Tramp*), both wearing conical party hats.

We'll have to accept the estimate of his age on faith, since, like others of his generation, Unding isn't sure when he was born. In the pre-literate days, parents would recall that a child was born when the hill rice was grown in such-and-such a location, or when the Japanese soldiers came, or when there was a big fire and the longhouse had to be moved.

When the government decided that everyone should have an identity card, Unding's parents fudged on the boy's age. He was (probably) 15, but they told the official he was 18 so he could get a passport. The official said, "don't push your luck" and made him 17. Since the identity card was issued in December, that's the de facto month of his birth.

But why did he need a passport? It relates to the right-of-passage *berjalai* that every able-bodied Iban young man undertakes. Berjalai can roughly be interpreted as a rite-of-passage journey, a leaving home to seek adventure, wealth, and a first tattoo. In the old days, a berjalai might result in the young man triumphantly returning to the longhouse with an enemy's head. Today a young Iban man might work in a timber camp or in the natural gas plant in Bintulu, or attend a university. Today he might return with a flat screen TV, an engineering degree, or a hard hat reading "Bechtel Saudi." Same game, different rewards. For his berjalai, Unding went to neighboring Brunei and brought back a souvenir that hangs on his wall — a small tapestry showing the Ka'aba in Mecca. I asked him why he displays that image, since he is not Muslim. "Just for the memory of the trip to [largely Muslim] Brunei," he said.

◇

I watched him at work.

One evening a family of four came to see Unding. A woman, 24 but looking older, had been debilitated by severe migraine headaches since the birth of her last child a year earlier. She had been to see Western doctors and had spent almost $1,000 in consultations and treatments. Seeing the manang was her last hope.

Unding chats with the woman for a while, then covers himself with a *pua* woven blanket. He holds two machete-like *parangs*, claps them together, and gives a hooting call. A TV in the next room broadcasts a game show. He removes the pua and chats with the woman and her husband. It's all very social, with a fair bit of joking.

Unding takes out his bag of amulets, bundled in a few tatty plastic bags. He puts special medicated oil on her forehead and rubs a stone he describes as Raja Genali (king of eels), which he found floating in the river following a dream-vison he had. She takes off her shirt, and he rubs her throat with a stone he claims is a meteorite. From a different bottle, which looks like it once contained cheap brandy, Unding rubs more oil on her back, legs, and stomach, all the while mumbling prayers. Then Unding's wife joins the group and serves sweet tea, and everybody has a good natter.

I later asked Unding what was wrong with the woman, who drove half an hour to Unding's longhouse. He explains that after giving birth she didn't follow the traditional belief to keep her lower back warm, so she is now suffering because spirits entered her body. The parangs are intermediary devices that asked the spirits to tell him what action to take.

When I arrived at the longhouse, I gave him gifts, much as in the West when you're invited to someone's house you bring a bottle of wine and a cheesecake: some fresh fish and vegetables from the Sri Aman market, tinned goods, biscuits for the kids, and a bottle of alcohol (I knew Unding himself doesn't drink much, but my guide Bayang Penguang explained that perhaps the alcohol could be brought out in the evening to lubricate a little longhouse party).

I also gave him a rather nice amulet of Ganesha, the Hindu elephant god, thinking he might be able to use it in his work. I explained its significance, told him it had been given to me by a Thai shaman, and made a case for its usefulness and universality. He seemed underwhelmed by the Ganesha and instead showed me his own magic charms — a wild boar's tooth, a chunk of petrified wood, a potion made of snake venom and herbs.

I collect protection fetishes for our house in Geneva, and I thought an Iban talisman couldn't hurt.

I asked whether his charms worked at a distance. Unding showed me some designs he had created (looking like swirls made with white fingerpaint) on the brown paper covers of school exercise books. He had a bunch of them, ready to go; obviously lots of people seek such homeowners' insurance. I bought one for $15 and hung it in the entryway of my house in Geneva; since then, we haven't been burgled, burned, or invaded by bad spirits.

In Search of…

ENLIGHTENMENT, CURIOSITIES, AND ULTIMATE MEANING

Is Life Really an Endless Karmic Loop?

A Friend Returns to His Birthplace on the Tibetan Plateau to Chase Personal Demons, While I Meet Two Ethnic Tibetan Girls Who Change My Life

Paul Spencer Sochaczewski
Tashi Gurung, returning to his birthplace in Upper Mustang.
Our goal: a three-day exorcism to rid the world of devils.

On a bluff in Kagbeni, at the entrance to the Kingdom of Mustang, a tantalizing sign warns: "Stop. You are now entering the restricted area of Upper Mustang."

This medieval-feeling town overlooks the wide, graveled, almost dry Kali Gandaki River. We gaze north toward distant villages where patches of green barley offer evidence of civilization in this arid landscape. We are about to traverse the ancient Salt Route that winds along the river's banks, connecting the lowlands of India and Nepal with the isolated mountain plateau of Central Asia. But before we can enter Upper Mustang, we first must show our trekking permits to the Nepalese authorities. Then we are through, and it feels like we have entered a hidden Narnia-like gate, a forbidden time warp. The snow-capped peaks of the Nilgiri mountains, part of the Annapurna range, are at our backs. We are headed north, toward Tibet.

For my friend Didier and me the trek to the Kingdom of Mustang in northern Nepal is the start of an adventure to a seldom-visited, exotic land.

For our friend Tashi Gurung, however, it is an emotional homecoming.

Tashi, a smiling, stocky Tibetan refugee who became a naturalized Nepalese citizen, was born some 40 years earlier in a nameless valley near Lo Manthang, the capital of Upper Mustang and our destination five days hence.

His family escaped from the Saga region in southwestern Tibet in 1958, just before the Chinese invasion. They wandered as semi-nomadic shepherds in the brown and ochre high-altitude deserts of Mustang with their flocks of yaks, sheep, and goats.

We hope to arrive for the beginning of the annual Tiji festival, a three-day exorcism to rid the world of devils.

Tashi has never seen Tiji. Since childhood, he has never seen his birthplace.

The reason for Upper Mustang's isolation is partly physical and mostly geopolitical. Following the Dalai Lama's flight to India from Tibet in 1959, a band of Tibetan guerrillas used Mustang as their center of anti-Chinese operations — Lo Manthang is just 25 kilometers (15 miles) from the border. To quell the uprising, the Chinese closed the Tibet-Mustang border in 1960 and pressured the Nepalese government to seal off Mustang from the rest of Nepal.

While a handful of researchers were allowed into the area, Mustang remained virtually closed to foreigners until March 1992. The government of Nepal, experimenting with a newly democratic outlook and eager to generate foreign exchange, decided that up to a thousand people a year could visit this isolated region.

A great part of Mustang's appeal to foreigners, of course, lies in the fact that it is hard to get to. There are no roads, no cars, no mountain bikes. To reach the area, visitors must walk, ride a pony, or charter a helicopter 42 kilometers (26 miles) from Kagbeni to Lo Manthang.

The other element of the appeal is that Mustang is one of the best places in the world to get close to Tibetan culture. Something about mysterious Tibet appeals to Westerners' longing for places that are dramatically different, especially when the esoteric culture, traditions, and history are complemented by a religion that preaches non-violence, worries about karma, and confidently believes in masked battles between the forces of good and evil.

⚜

What is it that attracts people to "forbidden" things?

Our natural curiosity? A self-testing? The desire to get away from our routine lives and see what kind of steel we have inside us?

The walking is strenuous, made tougher by the afternoon dust storms that originate in the lowlands and roar through the narrow Himalayan passes.

We suffer a bit — blisters, fatigue, jealousy about the seemingly more talented cook who accompanies the trekking group that always camps nearby, the broken rib of my friend Didier — but when we spend too much time complaining about grit in our eyes, we are pulled back to reality by remembering the epic crises recounted by Jon Krakauer in his book *Into Thin Air.* This account of the disastrous 1996 climbing season on Mount Everest includes the tale of Beck Weathers, a Texan climber who was several times given up for dead and abandoned outside in a blizzard on the roof of the world. Virtually blind, with severe frostbite (his nose had to be amputated, along with his right arm, the four fingers and thumb of his left hand, and parts of both feet), he somehow stumbled into camp, a frigid, immobile, unseeing ghost of a man. His refusal to die made our aches not worth complaining about.

I appreciate travel more when I have to push myself physically. It clears my mind. And, in a way, any strenuous journey (and I use the term to include spiritual and emotional travel) is a way of leaving home.

Travel writer Bruce Chatwin suggested that "'travel' is the same word as 'travail,' bodily or mental labor, toil, especially of a painful or oppressive nature, exertion, hardship, suffering, a journey." We travel to test ourselves, to cleanse, to rejuvenate. According to Chatwin, "This could be termed 'catharsis,' which is Greek for purging or cleansing." He notes that one controversial etymology of the word derives from *kathaírō*, to rid the land of monsters.

It made complete sense to arrive for Tiji and its casting out of demons.

⸺⬦⸺

As we approached Lo Manthang, we stood on a hill, looking at the centuries-old town that had required so much effort to reach. The late afternoon windstorm blew sand into our faces, and we protected ourselves with white prayer shawls.

"I can see now the kind of life my parents had," Tashi explains. "They had hard karma. Many obstacles to overcome."

⸺⬦⸺

Tiji seemed a fine opportunity to discuss philosophy.

"Tashi," I asked. "What's the meaning of life?"

Tashi is a Tibetan Buddhist. For him, life is a series of nearly endless loops, where your past ungraceful actions generally come back to haunt you.

He explained his spiritual operating system. "Do whatever you can according to your ability. The more you help people now, the

206

better it will be in the next life. Believe in god. Meditate."

"Tashi, you're making it too complicated," I replied. "Basically, life really is a beer commercial. You're only sure of going around once, so make the most of it."

But Buddhists, like the followers of so many other religions, believe that life is suffering. It's the Vince Lombardi school of religion — "no pain, no gain."

"Tashi, let me tell you the philosophy of the North American baby-boom tribe," I said. "Nobody on his death bed ever said, 'Gee, I wish I had stayed later in the office and made love less.'"

He responded with a universal aphorism. "You plant rice, you get rice."

To me, Tiji was simply a glorious spectacle. I admired monks clad in golden silk brocade robes, peaked leather hats, and yak-hair boots, who donned masks to enact the convoluted drama — part morality play, part epic. It was a bit like watching the Ring cycle — some spectacular moments mixed in with some tedious half hours. Monks tooted three-meter (10-foot) long copper trumpets and clanged cymbals against a background of a giant thangka painting half the size of a tennis court that hung in the town square. The noise and dust generated a feeling of a Tibetan country fair.

To Tashi, the events were sacred and profound.

The objective of Tiji is peace and brotherhood. Evil spirits are told to get out of town, and if the dancing monks have done their jobs properly, the demons of ignorance, arrogance, anger, and greed will have been effectively banned until next year's festival.

Tashi has his own demons to deal with.

He was stateless and lived much of his early life in refugee camps. He never studied beyond the ninth grade. And the toughest karma of all is that his son is wheelchair-bound with cerebral palsy.

I ask him whether anything can be done to help the boy.

"It's our karma," he explains. "My wife and I might have done bad things in a previous life, and our son might have done worse things."

Tashi explains that he went to see the Dalai Lama's doctor in Dharamsala, India, who confirmed a diagnosis of bad karma, but nevertheless suggested that the boy take traditional medicine. The karma, in this case, was stronger than the herbs, and the boy is still wheelchair-bound, unable to do anything for himself.

It's risky to be a smart-aleck when talking about another person's religion. "You know, Tashi, all these religions and philosophies that predict some kind of next-world-reward are based on a big gamble," I said. "They ask you to collect karma points but can't guarantee the outcome. You never know how many credits you need." Tashi looked at me strangely. "The only things you can be really sure about are that today you're alive and one day you won't be," I said in the annoying Brooklyn persona I sometimes drift into. "Therefore, it makes sense to live for today. Grab all the gusto you can while your plumbing's intact and before Alzheimer's sets in."

Being too polite to sneer, Tashi pretended to think about it.

❖

I reflected too. On the trail a few days earlier, we had stopped by the settlement of Gheling. By the village well, where the waterwheel was carved like a prayer wheel and carried offerings to heaven with each squeaky turn, we glimpsed a shy, disfigured girl.

That night her father brought her to the house where we were staying.

Her name was Tashi Angmo. Several years ago, the family *dzo* (a male hybrid between a yak and domestic cattle) gored her in the eye with his horn. The wound was never treated, and her face became infected and ugly.

Poor and healthy is tough. Poor and disfigured is really heavy karma. But who were we to interfere?

We asked the father why he hadn't sought medical help for the girl. With his daughter observing from the corner of the smoky room, he explained that they were poor, he had many children, and there weren't any doctors nearby anyway. With Tashi Gurung's help, we channeled a few hundred dollars through a local non-governmental organization. Tashi Angmo left her village for the first time and was brought to distant Kathmandu for surgery. Our hope was that she would be able to see out of the eye and maybe have a shot at a relatively normal life. Was it her karma to get gored by a dzo? Was it our joint karma for us to trek into her village while she was washing the family's clothes?

Lo Manthang is a distressed Shangri-La. It is a classical-style walled city, but because Raja Jigme Palbar Bista (the 25th king in a line of succession that began in 1380) has given permission for people to build outside the city limits, the town's fortress-like character has been modified. The streets and drains are shared by children, dogs, donkeys, and yaks. Dust permeates our clothes. The king's palace is a ramshackle affair, in need of an overhaul. Lo Manthang has been without its hydro-generated electricity for several years. No one is quite sure why, but basically something has broken, and no one has bothered to fix it. There is talk of constructing an airstrip, but no one expects it to happen soon. Medical care is basic — people with serious illnesses have to be carried to Jomson, 87 kilometers (54 miles) away, then flown to Pokhara or Kathmandu.

The flat stucco roofs are perfect places to dry yak dung, firewood, and thorny kindling, piles of which make fine nesting sites for finches. The three-story houses are as mysterious as the town itself, with narrow passageways and tiny hidden stairwells. The houses often have a large central courtyard, with rooms facing inward, resembling the inns featured in Chinese sword-fighting movies. It would be a great place to shoot a James Bond movie.

In summer, the people of Upper Mustang farm and herd livestock, but in the winter, they too wander far and seek new sights. Many people travel to India, where they successfully trade in woolen goods and cheap acrylic sweaters. Some shepherds head north into Tibet to trade sheep for Chinese goods. The donkey and yak caravans of the old Salt Route now carry a modest selection of manufactured goods, and at the Tiji festival the children show off their ability to blow big pink bubbles with their Dubble Bubble chewing gum. Many young men of Lo Manthang sport made-in-China counterfeit baseball caps of American sports teams — the Chicago Bulls, the New York Yankees, and the Miami Heat.

⚜

This business of karma kept coming back to me.

Tashi runs a charity, called the Himalayan Children's Foundation, which helps young Tibetan refugees get a good education. Through this group, I sponsor the education of Tsering Wangmo, an 11-year-old Tibetan refugee.

She's a great kid. Bright eyes, a little shy, cute as Bambi.

Once she wrote me a poem:

"King love Queen

Queen love baby

Baby love milk

But I love you."

More recently, showing off a bit, she wrote: "Please don't angry if there is some mistake in my letter and if my handwriting is bad. But I don't think that there is some mistake and handwriting is bad because no[w] I am 6 class."

Was it her karma to meet me through Tashi and get the education that might lead to a more successful life? Was it my karma to meet Tashi when two Canadian friends stopped by my Switzerland house one morning and invited me to go on a bike ride with this friendly man from distant mountains? Was it Tashi's karma to have a disabled son and to devote his life to helping others?

Tashi had no doubts about his belief. "If you do good things, you will get good things," he said.

Tashi collects karma points the way some people collect baseball cards. His version of karma implies a system of bonuses and penalties.

But I'm not sure anyone's keeping score. All I know is that synchronicity, to use Jung's term, is real. We met, after all.

I don't claim to understand much of this, but I accept it. In my wallet, I keep Tsering Wangmo's latest letter. "Many years gone I will be a good and best and intelligent girl in the world. That's all for today." She signed it: "I never forgot your kindness until you die."

On the afternoon of the third and final day of Tiji, the dancers leave Lo Manthang through the town's sole entrance gate, followed by several hundred people from Lo Manthang and surrounding villages and a sprinkling of tourists. At dusk, courtiers fire ancient muskets as a high lama shoots arrows at a puppet representing a demon. This is an important moment for the star Tiji dancer, Lama Nag Kunga, who meditated in isolation for three months prior to Tiji to purify his soul and obtain the inner strength needed to cast the demons out of this place. He's doing his best to ensure a better future for mankind.

The moment is oddly profane and sacred at the same time. I glance at Tashi, a short distance away, who watches intently. I don't disturb him.

Some 25 years later, I can report what happened to these friends. This business of karma continues to resonate.

Tashi emigrated to Vancouver, Canada, where his son, who requires constant attention, has better medical care and support.

Tsering Wangmo, my adopted goddaughter from Nepal, did indeed mature from "a good and best and intelligent girl in the world" into a similarly wonderful woman. She emigrated to the United States several years after her father won the green card lottery. The family lived for years in a cramped windowless basement apartment in Queens, New York, which is the most culturally diverse urban area in the world. (I recall a factoid that some 160 nationalities live along the number 7 subway line that runs through her neighborhood.) Tsering's parents got union jobs as housekeepers at the Hilton Hotel in midtown Manhattan, which guarantees a living wage, health care, and some social life with other people in New York — some, like them, just trying to get by in a new country. Tsering herself continued her studies and works as an executive assistant in a mid-town law firm. She lives in Connecticut with her husband (Tenzin, another Tibetan refugee) and has to commute an hour and half each way. Her parents now live nearby. She's got the cutest son imaginable, Jigdel, who loves the idea of space travel.

And Tashi Angmo, the village girl whose eye was damaged by a dzo? In 2015 I asked a friend, who happens to be an expert on the art and culture of Upper Mustang (I'm being modest on his behalf; he is *the* expert), if he could give her some money on my behalf the next time he visited Gheling. Coincidentally, or not, he was also my wife's PhD advisor at the School of Oriental and African Studies at the University of London. He easily found Tashi Angmo's family, who explained that she had become a Buddhist nun and is now studying at the Central University of Tibetan Studies in Varanasi, India (the same city where, by happy coincidence, Dechen Chuskit, the young woman from Ladakh, also studies — see the chapter "The Girl by the Side of the Road"). My friend obtained her email address (isn't globalization wonderful?), and I sent her a note. Six hours later she replied. She explained that at the request of her teacher she has changed her name to Ngawang Dechen and studies languages and Buddhist philosophy. She enjoys reading and has friends and a purpose. She sent a few selfies — her face is unscarred, and her eyes bright with life. I suspected she had much to teach me, a speculation that was confirmed when I visited her in Varanasi years later.

Jumping Through Buddhist Hoops in Burma

A Monk Explains Why It's Easy to Train Cats; Harder to Teach People

Paul Spencer Sochaczewski

Jumping cats in a Burmese monastery;
more than tourist entertainment.

"*C*ome on Brochette, jump through this hoop. Arnold Schwarzenegger can do it — it can't be that hard."

Our ginger cat in Geneva was doing what cats everywhere do — exactly what she felt like. Which at this moment was not jumping through a hoop.

I was trying to accomplish a similar *coup de persévérance*, which some monks in Burma have achieved: teaching cats parlor tricks. But Brochette wasn't buying it. What did the monks have that I didn't?

Lots of patience and an abundant supply of Friskies, as it turned out.

I was introduced to the famous Burmese jumping cats at the Nga Phe Kyaung monastery on Inle Lake.

The "jumping cat monastery" is a key stop for the trickle of tourists who visit Burma. There I met 25-year-old Venerable U Nanda, one of a dozen resident monks.

"It's easy to train cats," he said, somewhat reluctantly putting down his Burmese comic book. With a large dose of ennui, he explained that you simply start when they're kittens, scratch them under the chin, say *kon*, and when they leap reward them with kitty treats.

Obviously, it works. Every 30 minutes or so, when a group of visitors would accumulate, San Win, an assistant in the monastery, would put the cats through their paces.

"What's that one called?" I asked, pointing to a black-and-white tabby.

World-weary U Nanda explained "That's Leonardo di Caprio."

"And this one?"

"Demi Moore."

"Can I try?"

I held the wire hoop in front of Arnold Schwarzenegger, paradoxically one of the skinnier cats in the temple. I gave him a little nudge, ordered him to kon, and after he jumped, I rewarded him with a cat biscuit.

Meanwhile Tina Turner was curled up on my backpack, asleep. "Don't leave your things on the floor," U Nanda instructed. "She pisses everywhere."

After a while U Nanda started to open up. Perhaps he saw that since I wasn't going to go away, he might as well have a discussion. I was interested in Buddhist history; he was interested in conjugating English verbs.

Throughout our conversation, the 68-year-old abbot, Sayadaw Kite Ti, kept his distance and read a book. I don't read Burmese, but from the pictures of cowboys and horses, I was pretty sure it wasn't a religious text. He didn't glance up as visitors stuffed contributions into the offering boxes.

◇

A few days later, I trekked an hour up a butterfly-enhanced forest path on Mount Popa, arguably the most mystical hill in this most mystical of countries, to visit a 30-year-old hermit monk named Venerable U Sumana.

Hesitantly, I approached a cave and saw a young monk preparing a fire. I asked if I was disturbing him. Popping in unannounced suddenly seemed like a stupid idea — the last thing I wanted to do was get in the way of his accumulation of karma points. Nevertheless, for a recluse, U Sumana was remarkably outgoing. He had finished his morning prayers, he explained, and invited me to sit on the ledge and chat.

U Sumana took over the cave that had been the home of U Germany, a famous monk who had meditated in this damp, isolated ledge for 50 years. U Sumana had few possessions or clothes, and his diet consisted of a handful of rice and some vegetables. To me, such isolation, deprivation, and rigor would be purgatory. I like my diversions too much — the company of friends, Beethoven, a fine wine, golf, pizza. U Sumana, though, had a different view of his adopted home. "It's shady and cool. It's easy to get water. I'm in the middle of nature, and there's no one around to distract me from my prayers." He had bright eyes and an easy smile. He explained he had seen this cave in a dream and journeyed here from distant Mon state.

My rational, Cartesian mind was racing. "But what do you do all day?" I asked.

U Sumana explained simply: "I meditate." Sometimes sitting. Sometimes walking. He showed me his walking meditation. Very, very slowly, I tried to replicate his movement — I roll from my heel to the toe and hold the opposite foot in the air before placing it down. I concentrate on the action. He explains that this type of practice, called *zingyan shouk chin*, will clear my mind. It will help me to develop patience — just like training a cat, perhaps.

Back at Inle Lake, I sought out U Nanda. I felt I had unfinished business with the young monk, a feeling that there was more to him than a saffron-robed, feline-inclined impresario.

"You again," he said when I walked in. He wasn't hostile, but he wasn't overly welcoming.

I deliberately avoided the handful of curious visitors watching Brad Pitt and Michael Jackson leaping about on the linoleum. "Tell me about the temple," I asked. And he did. He showed me around the 160-year-old monastery, the oldest on Inle Lake. Proudly, he turned on overhead fluorescent lights so that I could better see the six two-meter (20 feet) tall lacquerware Buddha images, gilt-encrusted wooden statues, and carved pillars. He took me into the abbot's room to show me old, sacred Buddha images. After half an hour of looking through different eyes, for me, the monastery had evolved from a tourist site into a combination art museum and place of worship.

"What do you do?" he eventually asked me.

"I'm a journalist."

"Then tell people the monastery is more than cats. It's Buddha."

Just One More Ganesha
Is Collecting a Deep Psychological Need, Harmless Pastime, or Dangerous Obsession?

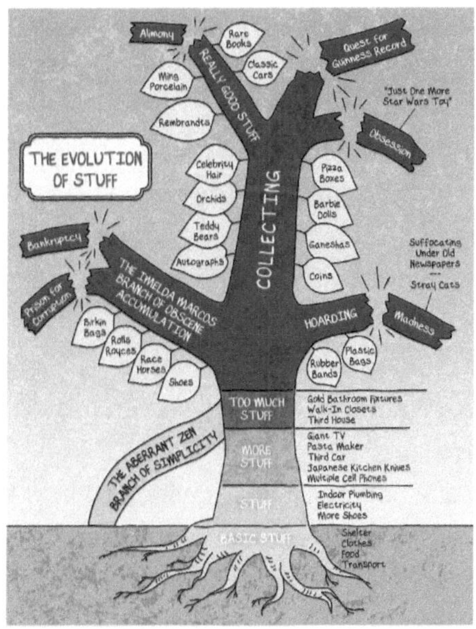

Illustration by Richard Sheppard, from Searching for Ganesha

Stuff can accumulate in different directions — valued
collections, dust-collecting junk, or life-obstructing rubbish.
Which direction is your stuff heading?

Barbie dolls. Porcelain chickens. Medieval armor. Stamps.
Toothpaste tubes. Fossils. Butterflies. Pizza boxes.

What is behind this widespread need to collect? Does quantity
matter? What do the psychoanalysts say — harmless pastime or
dangerous obsession?

* * *

I was a semi-nerdy kid growing up in northern New Jersey. Like many youngsters, I suppose, I collected stuff — baseball cards, rocks, and Native American arrowheads. (As an adult, I run across other men of my baby boom generation who collected these artefacts. Were there really so many arrowheads floating around in 1950s suburbia?)

My primary interest, though, was Roman coins. My favorite is a dupondius of Augustus and Agrippa celebrating the military victory against the combined forces of Mark Antony and Cleopatra at the Battle of Actium in 31 BCE. This coin, which cost me my modest weekly allowance, set the stage for Gaius Octavius to become Caesar Augustus, the first Roman emperor. The reverse shows a crocodile chained to a palm tree (pretty obvious Egyptian symbolism) under a stylized sun, with the legend COL NEM, indicating that it was minted in Nemausus (now Nimes, in southern France). I like to hold such coins and wonder what stories they could tell from 2,000 years ago.

I now collect statues, amulets, and images of Ganesha, the Hindu sweet-loving elephant-headed god who removes obstacles and supports writers.

I don't worship Ganesha. I'm fascinated by how he was created by Hindu marketing experts and retrofitted into the pantheon, and why he has become one of the world's favorite deities.

But behind my modest collection of some 150 Ganesha-related pieces lies the nagging question. Why? After all, I have just one mountain bike. One toaster. One garden hose. Surely one Ganesha should be enough?

⸻ ◆ ⸻

Everyone has stuff. Some of it is basic and essential to provide shelter, food, transport, and clothing. But stuff tends to expand. Essential stuff can too easily branch off into too-much stuff, which becomes clutter. The stuff might then grow a metaphorical tree limb and become an obsession, leading to hoarding. Or, in turn, the stuff might acquire emotional import and become a valued collection.

Sigmund Freud, the father of modern psychoanalysis, was what

I call a "magpie" collector. His consultation room in London, now a museum, was filled with some 3,000 varied antiquities, including a fifth-century BCE sphinx, a reproduction of Michelangelo's Dying Slave, African tribal sculptures, and plenty of phalluses (make of that what you will). Pride of place went to a bronze of the Greek goddess Athena, the female deity of wisdom, that he said protected him during his self-exile from Vienna.

Freud suggested that a chronic gatherer and organizer is locked in an anal-retentive mode, unwilling to let go, unable to touch his emotions. Writers Benjamin Poore and Harriet Agerholm described Freud's theory: "Our sense of ourselves — the 'I' that we each imagine ourselves to be — is made up of all the people and things we have once cherished and then lost or abandoned. Your identity is the accumulated heap of lost love objects. Which is to say, if you were to wander around your psyche, it might look rather like a room stuffed to the gunnels with dusty old artefacts, some tarnished, and now unloved, some recently rearranged, or polished; rather, in fact, like Sigmund Freud's study."

Werner Muensterberger, who has been described as an ethno-psychiatrist, amassed an important collection of African masks. He wrote: "Observing collectors, one soon discovers an unrelenting need, even hunger, for acquisitions. This ongoing search is a core element of their personality. It is linked to far deeper roots … which derives from a … sense memory of deprivation and a subsequent longing for substitution, closely allied with moodiness and depressive leanings."

Carl Jung felt that accumulations represent a collective, unconscious need to hoard "nuts and berries" once needed for survival by our early ancestors.

This psycho-babble can be tiring. Perhaps the answer is simple. Maybe a collection is a way of self-individuation, a way to say: *Hey, I'm different. I'm interesting. Attention must be paid.*

Does a collection need to be catalogued and put into taxonomic categories? Do we acquire a new piece based on whether it is rare (or expensive), fashionable, or beautiful? Does each object strike an emotional chord?

Can we judge the quality of a collection by numbers (Guinness World Record!)? The collector might be asking the smirking observer: *What do you think of my collection of garden gnomes (the world record is 1,600), umbrella sleeves (730), airline sickness bags (6,200), hot sauce (6,000 different bottles), pizza boxes (595), Barbie dolls (18,500), or toothpaste tubes (2,037)? Answer positively, and you can be my friend.*

But I'm not after quantity. Rama Shah of Mumbai has the world's largest collection of Ganesha-related items, some 18,181 pieces. I wouldn't trade even one of my pieces for his entire collection.

Each of my Ganesha statues tells me a story. And I, in turn, can tell a story about each one. How I acquired it. The aesthetic buzz I get by a statue's sinuous form, the intellectual zing I get when trying to unravel a figure's iconographic subtleties, or when I recall one of the countless Ganesha myths that have influenced the piece's intention and symbolism. With each piece, I recall the people who influenced me during my quest: *Just one more Ganesha, but it's got to be special.*

The collection hasn't taken over my life (or my house, to the relief of my wife). But it has made life more interesting and, as Ganesha should, opened a few important doors to adventures and friends.

But sometimes I wonder if collecting is a diversion, and I should pay more attention to the wisdom of the Dalai Lama, who wrote: "People assume that happiness stems from collecting things outside of yourself, whereas true happiness stems from removing things from inside of yourself."

Some day I will give away my Ganesha collection. But for now, my accumulation of fat, skinny, multi-armed, one-tusked, sitting, standing, reclining, and dancing Ganeshas simply gives me pleasure. That's something Freud never mentioned.

You Know Where That Coffee's Been?
Searching for the Perfect Dung-Delicious Civet Coffee

Paul Spencer Sochaczewski

A captive civet in Vietnam. Recently excreted civet-coffee dung,
Herry Setiawan at the blind-tasting of *kopi luwak* in Indonesia.

BUON MA THUOT, CENTRAL HIGHLANDS, VIETNAM

Oysters. Termites. Camembert. Snails. Snake blood. Brains. Broccoli.

On the long list of strange things that people voluntarily ingest, one might add civet coffee.

Civet coffee, called *café chon* in Vietnam and *kopi luwak* in Indonesia, is probably the only popular foodstuff that is consumed by people simply because it has passed through the digestive system of a wild animal.

It is also one of the world's most expensive delicacies. In 2008 upscale John Lewis department store in London made the evening "you'll love this next story" newscasts when it charged $100 for a cup of the brew served in the store's café.

I went to Vietnam and Indonesia to taste civet coffee, made moderately well-known when it appeared on Jack Nicholson's and Morgan Freeman's "bucket list" in the movie of the same name.

My journey isn't all that strange, actually.

First, I love coffee and admit to being a coffee snob. I appreciate a strong Italian espresso, straight up, no milk or sugar, always in a ceramic cup, never in paper or plastic.

Second, I like to eat strange things. I'm not a gurgitator in the sense of Takeru Kobayashi or Joey Chestnut or Sonya Thomas, folks who compete to see who can eat the most of something in a limited period. I'm an open-minded ingester. That has led me to enjoy foie gras, frogs, and horse in France. Chewy grilled goat testicles (called *satay torpedo* after the hoped-for physiological reaction when eaten by men) and *satay biawak* made from chicken-textured, somewhat fishy-tasting monitor lizard (good for skin disease, asthma, and, once again, male potency) in Java. Python, eaten in Borneo, tastes a bit like chicken; crocodile tastes like turtle; fermented Mongolian mare's milk called *kumis* tastes simply horrible. In Sulawesi, dog is gamy; paddy-field rats, sold by the roadside are palatable; and fruit bat is like honey-marinated wild boar. And *balut* in the Philippines, a duck-egg with embryo, is completely yucky, but said to help men's health. I've tucked into monkey in the Central African Republic; ants in Laos; and beetles, grasshoppers, and scorpions in Thailand. In Vietnam, my son and I ploughed through a nine-course cobra meal, which included the heart, blood, skin, flesh, and penis.

Civet coffee would be a piece of cake.

Except.

Except I was fully aware of the method by which civet coffee is produced.

◦────────◆────────◦

The life cycle of this beverage is the easy-target of sophomoric body-waste jokes.

Start with the wild Asian palm civet, *Paradoxurus hermaphroditus*, an attractive, wide-spread, raccoon-like, omnivorous, cat-sized animal with a pointy snout and a bushy tail.

The civet (sometimes mistakenly described as a "weasel" and often incorrectly called a "cat") likes the taste of ripe coffee berries, the cherry-sized fruit that contains the seed — what we call the coffee bean. According to the legend, which has almost certainly been enhanced by the marketing departments of the numerous companies producing civet coffee, the civet only selects the ripest, juiciest fruits. The critter nibbles away the coffee-berry flesh (which tastes vaguely like cherries, actually) and swallows the seed. Then the gustatory transformation takes place: The civet's digestive enzymes impart a rich, chocolaty essence to the coffee while softening the hard edges. A day later, the flavor-enhanced seeds emerge as civet-coffee feces, shaped like a skinny pine cone and resembling a roughly-made peanut-coated chocolate bar. The seeds are collected, cleaned, roasted, and sold for ridiculous amounts of money.

They resulting brew is said to taste terrific.

◦────────◆────────◦

I was invited to try civet coffee in the middle-class home of Mai Van Kien, in the town of Buon Ma Thuot in the Central Highlands of Vietnam. Kien, a coffee trader and farmer, is one of the happiest and most vigorous 80-year-olds I've met. "This will taste great," he suggested pouring hot water into the ubiquitous Vietnamese coffee filter device that has been likened to a "top hat" and technically described as a "tin coffee thingy."

I tasted a brew that was strong, earthy, flavorful, nutty, and round. Kien, who fought with South Vietnamese forces in what in Vietnam is called "the American war," was imprisoned and "re-educated" by the North Vietnamese victors for a year after the conflict for re-education. Today he is at peace. He sat with Nguyen Thi My, his 70-something wife, laughing and never moving far from each other, one of the happiest and most touchy-feely couples I've seen. His house was filled with clean-potted plants, framed family photos, an aquarium, and a big TV. On the front porch, next to coffee drying on the ground, stood a motorcycle. Kien revealed his secret for what he termed his "wealthy life." "Loyal marriage, eat lots of vegetables, get to sleep on time, be careful." Coffee didn't fit into his recipe for happiness, though; when I visited, Kien and his wife drank tea.

But the problem with drinking coffee with Kien is that small-scale coffee producers like him, as well as the big Vietnamese manufacturers, regularly add flavorings to their coffee. Was that chocolate-taste on my tongue the result of the civet's gut juices working their magic, or was it added by roasting the beans over a cocoa-wood fire? What about the slight buttery aftertaste? The peppery tang? The sweetness — natural or a touch of sugar? And was that a hint of red wine?

Some large Vietnamese coffee factories go beyond flavoring and have become civet coffee alchemists. Market-leading Vietnamese coffee company Trung Nguyen manufactures an artificial brew that they describe as "produced by an enzyme treatment process that mimics the changes produced in the coffee beans by the civet and which releases a whole spectrum of flavors that normally lie dormant." Their "weasel-enzyme" technique is secret and has the benefit, Ma Son Tung, the company's market development manager notes, "of not requiring any involvement from the animals."

While I was imbibing civet coffee, I had a nagging question.

Who was the first person to have the audacity to go to the trouble of making and drinking civet coffee?

None of the farmers I spoke with in Vietnam or Indonesia could cite long-standing cultural use of civet coffee. Dang Xuan Vu, whose family has grown coffee for generations, said "yes, the old folks said that weasel coffee is the best, but up until recently, we had never tried it." Some farmers say café chon is excretory ecstasy; other farmers won't touch the stuff, reflecting the view of a farmer I met in Vietnam who disdains it because it's "made from poo."

Dang Xuan Vu has a plausible explanation. He suggests French or Dutch colonial plantation owners forbade their Vietnamese and Indonesian workers from drinking the valuable coffee they harvested, so the poor farmers had no option but to clean and roast the unwanted feces-enrobed beans that had been excreted by the civet. Word got back to the European masters that this was a good brew, then the marketing folks took over.

But still, who might have been Civet Coffee Drinker Number One? Was he or she a lateral-thinking peasant hero who genuinely bought into the idea that civets only select the finest coffee berries? Or just some desperate, curious, anti-establishment goof-off who said, "what the hell?"

Of course, there's a lot of cultural relativism in considering what constitutes acceptable food. The French eat horse, Americans never touch the stuff. Many Europeans relish fresh oysters, but a lot of Asians gag at the slimy mollusk. Southeast Asians love sticky and stinky durian, while Westerners won't approach a fruit that smells like eating strawberries and cream in a badly maintained public toilet. Is it texture? Taste? A cultural concept of what constitutes food?

My self-inflicted food prohibitions are based less on taste-appeal and more on conservation right-mindedness. I try to boycott Chinese restaurants that serve shark's fin, octopus, and coral reef fish. I've refused to eat bear. Chimpanzee is a no-no. Birds' nest soup, though, made from the saliva of swiftlets, is ok (but tasteless).

⊷••••••◆••••••⊶

Civets have their own problems — civet coffee might disappear because the civets themselves are disappearing.

The Asian palm civet, while commonly found in forests and rural areas in South and Southeast Asia, is a protected species in Vietnam. The animal is becoming scarce in some areas, ironically a victim of farmers cutting down forests to plant coffee. The other problem is that civets are pests and eat chickens and ducks, so farmers often have little compunction about shooting the critters. There's an animal rights issue too: Wild civet dung is awfully hard to find, and Indonesian and Vietnamese entrepreneurs breed wild-caught civets in cramped and dirty cages and force feed them coffee cherries. And the coup-de-civet is that the flesh tastes pretty good. It is said to taste terrific when roasted by farmers in a thatched-roof farmhouse. And it is said to taste even better when fried with garlic and lemongrass at the Binh Minh restaurant in Dak Mil, some 70 kilometers (43 miles) outside Buon Ma Thuot, in the heart of the Central Highlands coffee-growing region. The owner, a taciturn Chinese-Vietnamese businessman, admitted that he fries several dozen animals a week. But he clammed up when we asked too many questions. After all, civets are protected in Vietnam, and he fully realizes his business is illegal. Nevertheless, civet's on the menu, costing roughly seven-times pork, and selling for about $5 per plate.

⌖

Lots of people will offer you civet coffee. Is it genuine? Has it been enhanced? Faux-civet coffee wasn't my goal. I sought the real deal. I needed a control sample, a somewhat-scientific taste test in which I could compare civet coffee with "normal" coffee from the same plantation, with both samples prepared in the same way. A double-blind experiment.

Virtually every journalist, every gee-whiz wide-eyed travel blogger, every oh-so-daring social media influencer who writes about civet coffee gets it wrong. Virtually all reports about the taste of civet coffee are nonsense because the taster imbibes a single cup of the brew presented to him or her by, usually, a café barista or company shill. The journalist has nothing to compare it against.

The only way to accurately taste civet is to set up a blind taste testing pitting "normal" and "civet" coffee made from beans from the same plants, harvested from the same precise location, and brewed in exactly the same way.

I organized three such blind tastings.

First, I asked my friend Dang Xuan Vu for help.

Dang Xuan Vu, my guide during my search for the last elephant hunter in Vietnam, understands my quirks and is patient with my endless questions. He understood my frustration with tasting civet coffee in isolation. The brew might taste sweet, soft, round, full, chocolatey, or a hundred other wine-like adjectives. But is it sweeter, softer, rounder, fuller, and chocolatier than normally produced coffee that has never seen the inside of a civet's gut?

Vu, whose family owns a three-hectare (eight-acre) coffee plantation in Vietnam's Central Highlands, mailed me two vacuum sealed packets of coffee. The first was "normal" Robusta, the cheap rustic coffee grown locally. The second, roasted and ground in exactly the same way, was Robusta civet coffee.

I prepared both samples the same way, in a French press, and served the coffee to guests at a dinner party in Bangkok. Almost unanimously, my friends and I preferred the civet coffee, using phrases like "rounder," "sweeter," and "drinkable" to describe the taste. That doesn't mean that they would have preferred civet coffee to, say an Illy espresso, but they preferred civet coffee to the "normal" brew.

The second tasting, in Ho Chi Minh City, was put together by friends in the coffee business, with Arabica coffee from the same Central Highlands farm, the only difference being one sample was café chon and one was "normal" coffee. Both were roasted and prepared in the same way.

I found it easy to distinguish between the two samples, with the café chon being richer in flavor and less stringent.

For an even more sophisticated tasting, I flew to Medan, North Sumatra, a city of 2 million which hadn't changed much in the 30 years since I had first visited. Half an hour out of town, I was welcomed to the head office of P.T. Coffindo, which prides itself as providing kopi luwak made only from wild civets that live in the coffee plantations, not in cages.

Coffindo executives agreed to set up a comparative tasting of kopi luwak (which in Indonesian means "coffee civet") and "normal" coffee prepared with the same beans that were identically grown in the same plantation but which hadn't had the benefit of a civet's intestinal juices.

Herry Setiawan is a certified coffee taster working with Coffindo; one diploma hanging on the wall of his glass-enclosed tasting room identifies him as a "star cupper," which means he is qualified to judge international coffee competitions. Like his counterparts in the fields of wine production and chocolate manufacturing, his palate and sense of smell are highly sensitive.

Using jargon reminiscent of wine tasting, Setiawan suggested I pay attention to "body, acidity, sweetness, flavor, color, and aroma."

Setiawan set out several small bowls, half filled with normal coffee, half with kopi luwak. All the samples were high-quality Arabica from the same plantation in Aceh, North Sumatra.

First, we examined and sniffed the dry coffee that Setiawan had just roasted and ground. Already I could detect a difference: The normal coffee was earthy, had an after-the-rain freshness, and tones of nuttiness and milk chocolate. The kopi luwak, on the other hand, had distinct notes of dark chocolate, caramel, and something I couldn't quite identify. "Forest flowers?" Setiawan suggested.

He then added mineral water that had boiled and allowed to cool to 93 degrees Celsius (200 degrees Fahrenheit). He was very specific about the temperature. Setiawan slowly stirred the brew and sniffed the back of the spoon. The aroma was enhanced by the addition of hot water, and in the kopi luwak, I smelled a note of something unexpected. "Green tea?" I asked. "Good nose," Setiawan said.

Then came the tasting. Setiawan showed me how to half-fill the spoon, loudly slurp it into my mouth with a good intake of air, swish it around my tongue, and spit it into a red plastic pail. The normal coffee was nutty and earthy, very fresh. The kopi luwak, on the other hand, had distinct notes of chocolate, caramel, and flowers. It was stronger, rounder.

———◇———

Although kopi luwak and café chon account for a small percentage of coffee production in Indonesia and Vietnam, the markups are phenomenal. P.T. Coffindo sells a kilogram (35 ounces) of roasted kopi luwak beans for around $800, about 40 times the price of their "normal" Arabica. But the market is getting crowded, and I wonder how much demand there really is. Maybe the marketing folks should be more adventurous with their branding. I wonder whether a product called "Excretory Ecstasy" or "Fecal Fabulous" or "Dung Delicious" would boost sales.

I'll continue to search for the perfect fecalicious kopi luwak. But sometimes I feel the need to expand my gustatory horizons and take on new challenges. My Australian friends swear I'll love Vegemite.

Is Immortality a Binomial? Or a Baby?

People Go to Exceptional Lengths to Avoid Dying and Disappearing

Adobe Stock/Maizal

Having a plant or animal named after you can lead to immortality. But the honor can be double-edged: The Rafflesia, named after the founder of modern Singapore, is simultaneously the world's largest, but also the world's smelliest, flower.

GENEVA, SWITZERLAND

I'm going to die. I don't know when or under what circumstances. It will be my last quest, one I won't be able to write about. If I get a chance, I will probably grumble, fight, and curse. But some people refuse to accept that, for them, death exists. So, how might immortality work?

A few people are, let's say, big. They are part of popular history and myth. Historians, pundits, and keen fans ponder what legacy an

231

athlete, artist, serial killer, or politician might leave. Hero? Bum? Tyrant? Opportunist? Con-man? Genius? Greatest of All Time?

But most people lead lives that are privately important while they are alive but are forgotten after one or two generations of their death. These are the mass of people who simply go to work, have a family, give to charity, and don't kick dogs. Ho-hum, as far as immortality-by-achievement is concerned. Their memory will be recorded in a few desiccating misremembered anecdotes, a few rapidly disintegrating photos, a memento or two, and a moss-encrusted gravestone with some dates and maybe a heart-warming platitude.

Creative genius is one path. If you were Verdi, you could write an opera. If you were Shakespeare, you could write unforgettable plays. Homer's name is likely to last for many more centuries, as will Leonardo da Vinci's and Valmiki's.

Some people seek a quick fix to ensure immortality. One might:
- instruct your subjects to locate the Elixir of Life (Qin Shi Huang, first emperor of a unified China, c. 210 BCE, died after ingesting cinnabar — mercury sulfide).
- search for the Fountain of Youth (16th-century conquistador Juan Ponce de León).
- create the Philosopher's Stone (15th-century Vincenzo Cascariolo ingested a potion composed of barite, powdered coal, and iron; he didn't live forever, but in the attempt, he created the world's first glow-in-the-dark substance).
- ingest the vomit of cholera patients (19th-century physiologist Charles-Édouard Brown-Séquard) or drink the blood of three young boys (15th-century Pope Innocent VIII).
- sell your soul to the devil (Faust).
- keep yourself cryogenically frozen, to be defrosted once a cure has been found for the illness that killed you (According to *Sports Illustrated*, the body and head of baseball legend Ted Williams were frozen for this purpose.)

Or one might subscribe to a religion that promises a happy forever-after life. *Good news! There is life after death!* This concept is enshrined in the popular euphemism "passed away," used when someone dies. The hard-consonant verb "to die" is an abrupt, final, drum-roll thwack, a guillotine irreversibly severing a human being from his or her humble existence. But the softer, more open-ended verb "passed away" is a fluffy cloud floating on a gentle breeze. It implies that physical death is merely a stumble, a detour, an optimistic opening of a door to something *else*. Countless individuals who do not consider themselves religious believe in an afterlife of some type. And this promise is one of the main marketing pitches of most faiths. It uses circular logic to convince the believer that he or she is a sinner and will suffer a really unpleasant afterlife unless the mendicant follows the rituals mandated by the priests, gives generously to the religious bureaucracy, and asks for forgiveness. The church is, in effect, selling a form of immortality insurance. *We can't promise it, but trust us, we wear funny clothes, chant in obscure languages, hang out in ornate temples, and read from holy texts.* And who's to say they're not right? Who's to say whether we are more than our corporeal body, whether we possess something ethereal, eternal, and beautiful called a soul, and that when we die that immortal soul can reside everywhere or nowhere.

Another possible route to immortality is to get something biological named after you and hope that it is not a "synonym" — a species thought to be new but that, in fact, had already been described and named by someone else. This fate happens to some 3,000 "new" species annually.

Since the beginning of taxonomic classification, hundreds, perhaps thousands of people — the virtuous as well as the vicious — have had creatures named in their honor.

- Alfred Russel Wallace so honored the White Rajah of Sarawak, writing: "This species [Rajah Brooke birdwing butterfly], which was then quite new, and which I named after Sir James Brooke, [Wallace called it *Ornithoptera Brookeana*, now *Trogonoptera brookiana*] was very rare ... [and] one of the most elegant species known."

- Olof Rudbeck gave Carl Linnaeus his first job. In thanks, Linnaeus, who, in 1753, devised the standard binomial classification for cataloging life on Earth, saw to it that Rudbeck became a flower, *Rudbeckia hirta*, the American black-eyed susan. Linnaeus wrote to his professor: "So long as the earth shall survive, and as each spring shall see it covered with flowers, the Rudbeckia will preserve your glorious name."

- Hugh Hefner, of *Playboy* magazine fame, financed research that identified the smallest and rarest of three known marsh rabbit subspecies. Found only in the Florida Keys, the animal has been named *Sylvilagus palustris hefneri*.

- Sir Stamford Raffles, credited as being the founder of modern Singapore, was honored to have the world's largest flower named after him: Rafflesia. The victory was perhaps Pyrrhic, since the parasitic Rafflesia is sometimes called the "stinking corpse lily," the world's smelliest flower.

- Wikipedia has a page devoted to creatures named after celebrities (who compiles this stuff? Bless them). Some highlights of such eponyms: *Agra schwarzeneggeri* is a species of carabid beetle from Costa Rica with a bicep-like middle femora. Frank Zappa has at least three creatures bearing his name, including a jellyfish. George W. Bush, Dick Cheney, Donald Rumsfeld, and Darth Vader have beetles named after them. SpongeBob SquarePants has a musky-smelling fungus from Malaysia. Mozart, Beethoven, John Lennon, Mick Jagger, Keith Richards, Elton John, Sid Vicious, Beyoncé, Taylor Swift, and Freddy Mercury all have their creatures, as do Buddha and Confucius (a feathered dinosaur). King Charles III has a frog while David Attenborough has had his name given to more than 50 newly discovered species. A spider has been named after the baseball pitcher Dizzy Dean;

it uses a sticky ball on the end of a thread to catch its prey.
Marilyn Monroe is honored by *Norasaphus monroeae*, a fossil
trilobite with an hourglass-shaped glabella, while Greta Garbo
has a wasp described as "a solitary female."

Every year some 18,000 new species are identified, about half of
which are insects. In 2021 the Natural History Museum in London
identified 552 new critters, all in search of a name. Many have long
gone extinct: a vegetarian dinosaur relative of crocodiles, fossilized
moss and algae, as well as spiders trapped in amber.

But a vigorous debate rages among taxonomists, the self-ap-
pointed "keepers of the scientific names," about whether to name
species after unsavory individuals. Consider a rare, blind cave beetle
that, according to Doug Yanega, an entomologist at the University
of California, Riverside, "eats anything smaller and weaker than
it." It was discovered in 1932 in a cave in modern-day Slovenia by
a naturalist named Vladimir Kodric. Oskar Scheibel, an Austrian
railway engineer whose hobby was coleopterology, the study of
beetles, agreed the insect represented a new species. He reneged on
his promise to name the beetle after Kodric and, in 1937, registered
it as *Anophthalmus hitleri*, writing: "Given to Reich Chancellor Adolf
Hitler as an expression of my admiration."

Similar arguments in favor of changing scientific names include
Hypopta mussolini, a Libyan moth, and Hibbertia, a genus of Australian
guinea flowers christened after Geroge Hibbert, a patron of botany
who got rich on the trans-Atlantic slave trade.

I wonder what the taxonomic future will hold for a thumb-
nail-sized moth with pale blond head scales and small genitalia.
Alan Burdick, writing in the *New Yorker*, says "It could be mistaken
for a dishevelled roach." In 2017 scientists named this cross-border
critter, found only in California and northern Mexico, after the 45th
president of the United States: *Neopalpa donaldtrumpi*.

But even if you are a living saint, a purveyor of frothy happiness,
a generous philanthropist, or simply a down-to-earth citizen, you
now have no chance of having a North American bird named after

you. Beginning in 2024, the American Ornithological Society will begin to rename some 70 to 80 species found in the US and Canada that carry an individual's name, and new bird species will be identified solely by habitats and characteristics.

Some of the names to be changed recognize explorers and legitimate scientists, such as Lewis's woodpecker (*Melanerpes lewis*), named after Meriwether Lewis, who first described the bird during his exploration of a vast swathe of western United States acquired in the 1803 Louisiana Purchase.

However, several of these soon-to-be-changed bird names honor unsavory characters. Townsend's warbler (*Setophaga townsendi*) is named after John Kirk Townsend, a 19th-century ornithologist and collector who is said to have robbed Indigenous graves of skulls. Scott's oriole (*Icterus parisorum*) is named after US Civil War General Winfield Scott, who oversaw the forced relocation of Indigenous peoples in 1838 that eventually became known as the Trail of Tears. Audubon's shearwater (*Puffinus lherminieri*) is named after John James Audubon, the famous French-American naturalist, wildlife illustrator, and slave owner. (The eponymous National Audubon Society, a leading US bird conservation organization, has rejected pressure and decided not to change its name.)

But the easiest and most lasting route to immortality is through a practice engaged in by some 350,000 people daily. Make a baby. Genetic immortality is a sure-fire path to ensure that at least some part of you will live on after you die.

I will never write a symphony like Beethoven. I will never achieve a physical exploit like Edmund Hillary and Tenzing Norgay, who first summited Mount Everest. I have written a bunch of books, but they are likely to be increasingly ignored considering that roughly 4 million books are published each year.

But I have a son, David. And a granddaughter, Ranya Apsara. Through them, hopefully, the quests will continue.

Praise for Paul's Other Books

"LOOK HERE, SIR, WHAT A CURIOUS BIRD"
SEARCHING FOR ALI, ALFRED RUSSEL WALLACE'S
FAITHFUL COMPANION
Explorer's Eye Press, Geneva, 2023
ISBN: 987-2-940573-41-7

Alfred Russel Wallace was one of the greatest naturalists and explorers of the Victorian era.

In Borneo in 1855 he hired a 15-year-old young man named, simply, Ali, who evolved into a reliable camp manager and preparer of bird skins. Ali was also an expert bird collector, and, by some accounts, was responsible for shooting some 5,000 of the 8,050 bird specimens Wallace collected. This is Ali's "enhanced biography."

Sochaczewski argues that Wallace would not have been as successful as he was without the support of Ali, whom he described as his "faithful companion." The author also examines the near-impossible challenge of finding a unique "truth." He offers imagined conversations and informed speculations and suggests we each have an "Ali" who has helped us along our life journey but who hasn't received adequate recognition or thanks.

"A new literary genre. Remarkable creativity combining solid scholarship, personal memoir, good heart and hearty humor; delicious speculation; soul-touching imagined scenarios; and a plenitude of cartoons and photos. A splendid work of innovative history writing."
— *James Clad, Board of Supervisors, Library of Congress*

A CONSERVATION NOTEBOOK
EGO, GREED, AND OH-SO-CUTE ORANGUTANS — TALES FROM A HALF-CENTURY ON THE ENVIRONMENTAL FRONT LINES
Explorer's Eye Press, Geneva, 2022
ISBN: 978-2-940573-39-4

This highly personal volume from the former head of Creative Services for WWF International wanders the world in search of conservation successes and failures, heroes and villains. The book contains no finger-wagging lectures, not too many depressing statistics, and no easy solutions. It is a collection of curious encounters and outlying ideas reflecting five decades of work in the nature conservation wonderland, linked by the theme that nature is too important to ignore.

"An endearing inspiration and a wonderful tribute to the movements and characters behind modern conservation."
— *Tobgay Sonam Namgyal, former head of the Bhutan Trust Fund for Environmental Conservation*

"A must-read for all those involved in the race to save the planet."
— *Mark Halle, former director of IUCN, founding director of Better Nature*

"Don't read this book seeking glib solutions. But do read it, please, to get a human, and frequently moving story about how conservation works in the real world."
—*James Clad, former bureau chief South and Southeast Asia,* Far Eastern Economic Review, *former U.S. deputy assistant secretary of defense for Asia*

SEARCHING FOR GANESHA
COLLECTING IMAGES OF THE SWEET-LOVING, ELEPHANT-HEADED HINDU DEITY EVERYBODY ADMIRES
Explorer's Eye Press, Geneva, 2021
ISBN: 978-2-940573-37-0

Ganesha, the Hindu elephant-headed god, is among the most-treasured of all deities. In this innovative book Sochaczewski explores why he collects Ganesha images (some 80 objects from his collection are shown in museum-quality photos), examines the psychology of collecting, and recounts personal adventures in his 40-year quest for just-one-more Ganesha statue. He describes the book as "a personal travel adventure with zero religious intent."

"A treasure. Part intellectual homage, part personal journey, part sheer whimsy. A noble tip of the hat to one of the world's favorite gods."
— *Ro King, chair, Global Heritage Fund and chair emeritus, Indonesian Heritage Society*

"Sochaczewski's deep knowledge is matched only by his humanistic spirit, humor, and modesty that runs through the book. Ganesha aside (because I will readily admit that the author's mastery of the subject is far greater than mine), his acute questioning of the desire to collect should become mandatory reading for budding museum professionals."
— *Danien Kunik, curator for Asian collections, MEG-Musée d'ethnographie de Genève*

EARTHLOVE
CHRONICLES OF THE RAINFOREST WAR
Explorer's Eye Press, Geneva, 2020
ISBN: 978-2-940573-34-9

EarthLove, a satiric Borneo eco-adventure, chronicles the history of the global conservation movement and exposes battles pitting ego and greed versus noble intentions. Who has the power to stop the rape of the tropical rainforests? Is there hope for the people of the rainforest? For the orangutans? For the forces of good to outlast the armies of evil?

"Scents of Carl Hiaasen, Edward Abbey, and Tom Wolfe combined into a unique voice of darkly comic fictional truth."
— *Simon Lyster, chairman, Conservation International, UK*

"An absolute delight, EarthLove reveals the dark, and deliciously satirical, underbelly of modern conservation."
— *Nigel Barley, author of* The Innocent Anthropologist, *former curator for Southeast Asia, British Museum*

DEAD, BUT STILL KICKING
ENCOUNTERS WITH MEDIUMS, SHAMANS, AND SPIRITS
Explorer's Eye Press, Geneva, 2019
ISBN: 978-2-940573-32-5

In this innovative work of personal journalism, Sochaczewski — a self-described Skeptical Spiritualist — creates the Three Tenets of Spiritualism while travelling to Indonesia, Myanmar, the United Kingdom, and Switzerland to speak with spirits of dead folks. He gets a personal mandate from Moses, speaks with Alfred Russel Wallace about his relationship with Charles Darwin, encounters a vengeful female vampire ghost, and converses with nature spirits.

"Enlightening. A noble companion volume to my own books on spiritualism."
— *Spirit of Arthur Conan Doyle*

"A brave attempt to understand the widening gyres."
— *Spirit of W.B. Yeats*

Exceptional Encounters
Enhanced Reality Tales from Southeast Asia
Explorer's Eye Press, Geneva, 2018
ISBN: 978-2-940573-29-5

Exceptional Encounters takes the seeds of true events and applies the classic fiction writer's aerobic exercise by asking: What if? These enhanced-reality fabulations draw the reader into tales of just over-the-rainbow Asian kindness, greed, passion, and dreams.

"A touch of George Orwell for our challenging times."
— *Robin Hanbury-Tenison, founder of Survival International*

"At turns outrageous, thoughtful, and darkly satirical. Pushes the frontier of personal travel literature into a new dimension."
— *Simon Lyster, chairman World Land Trust*

REDHEADS
A Comic Eco-Thriller Set in Borneo
Explorer's Eye Press, Geneva, 2016
ISBN: 978-2-940573-18-9

In the middle of a Borneo rainforest, a band of near-naked Penan tribesmen, encouraged by a similarly clothes-challenged renegade Swiss shepherd, blockade a logging truck. Nearby, a researcher studying orangutans is threatened with being thrown out of her study site unless she can reach a delicate compromise with the powerful minister of the environment. Meanwhile, a few identity-confused orangutans seek their own methods of survival.

Will the threatened homeland of people and orangutans survive?

"*Redheads* does for the struggle to save the rainforests of Borneo what *Catch-22* did for the struggle to stay alive in World War II."
— *Daniel Quinn, author of* Ishmael

"A visceral jungle morality play. Free-thinking, intelligent, and irreverent, reminds me of a Kurt Vonnegut thriller."
— *Benedict Allen, author of* Into the Crocodile's Nest:
Journey Inside New Guinea

An Inordinate Fondness for Beetles
Campfire Conversations with Alfred Russel Wallace
Explorer's Eye Press, Geneva, 2017
ISBN: 978-2-940573-25-7

An Inordinate Fondness for Beetles follows the Victorian-era explorations of Alfred Russel Wallace through Southeast Asia.

Sochaczewski examines themes about which Wallace cared deeply and interprets them through his own filter with layers of humor, history, social commentary, and sometimes outrageous personal tales.

"The rhythm and magic of a verbal fugue. A new category of nonfiction — part personal travelogue, part incisive biography, part unexpected traveller's tales."

— *Dato Sri Gathorne, author of* Mammals of Borneo

"As if I had boarded a time machine. A revelation of Wallace's insights interwoven with Sochaczewski's unique view of the world and our place in it."
— *Thomas E. Lovejoy, professor at George Mason University, president of the Amazon Biodiversity Center*

SHARE YOUR JOURNEY
MASTERING PERSONAL WRITING
Explorer's Eye Press, Geneva, 2016
ISBN: 978-2-940573-15-8

Share Your Journey is a generously illustrated and easy-to-use handbook for people who want to write their personal stories. The book's Ten Writing Tips gives writers the techniques professional authors use to write memoirs and travel stories that connect with readers and editors.

"This is a lifetime's wisdom, offered by a pro. Put *Share Your Journey* next to *The Elements of Style* by Strunk and White — they'll be the only two writing books you'll need."

— *Thomas Bass, author of* The Spy Who Loved Us

"*Share Your Journey* is to good writing as *Joy of Cooking* is to good food. It's smart, fun, and every page contains nuggets of essential advice."

— *Gary Goshgarian, professor of creative writing, Northeastern University*

CURIOUS ENCOUNTERS OF THE HUMAN KIND
TRUE ASIAN TALES OF FOLLY, GREED, AMBITION, AND DREAMS

Explorer's Eye Press, Geneva, 2016
Southeast Asia ISBN: 978-2-940573-13-4
Indonesia ISBN: 978-2-940573-03-5
Himalaya ISBN: 978-2-940573-07-3
Borneo ISBN: 978-2-940573-10-3

A five-volume series — Myanmar (Burma), Southeast Asia, Indonesia, Himalaya, and Borneo — containing true stories based on Sochaczewski's 50 years of living and exploring in curious corners of Asia. This is Asia as you've probably never imagined, full of memorable people, startling happenings, and unexpected moments of humanity and introspection, giddiness and solemnity, avarice and ambition.

⁓

"The spirit of Kipling in contemporary Asian journalism. This collection is essential reading for anyone who wishes to pass beyond even the unbeaten track, right to the heart of Asia."

— *John Burdett, author of* Bangkok Asset

"The humanity of Somerset Maugham, the adventure of Joseph Conrad, the perception of Paul Theroux, and a self-effacing voice unique his own."
— *Gary Braver, bestselling author of* Tunnel Vision

DISTANT GREENS
GOLF, LIFE, AND SURPRISING SERENDIPITY
ON AND OFF THE FAIRWAYS
Explorer's Eye Press, Geneva, 2016
ISBN: 978-2-940573-21-9

Distant Greens travels to the highest golf course in the world, where breathless Tibetan precepts come face to face with the Indian military. To a golf course in the Amazon rainforest, near the source of rubber, which revolutionized the game. To the Middle Kingdom, to examine claims that it was the Chinese who invented golf.

More than an insightful personal travelogue, *Distant Greens* also delves into the soul of the sport and shows how golf can be a force for nature conservation.

"An intimate golfing tour that travels to all corners of the planet and brings us into the heart, mind, and soul of the game that we all love."

— *Rick Lipsey,* Sports Illustrated

SOUL OF THE TIGER
SEARCHING FOR NATURE'S ANSWERS IN SOUTHEAST ASIA
Jeffrey A. McNeely and Paul Spencer Sochaczewski
University of Hawai'i Press, Honolulu, 1995
ISBN: 0-82481-669-2

One recent reviewer noted: "Age has not diminished the value of this book; it remains a classic in the genres of both conservation and travel literature."

Soul of the Tiger identifies the four "eco-cultural revolutions" that have dramatically changed the face of Southeast Asia and suggests a fifth revolution that could lead to a new sustainable relationship between people and nature.

"One revealing, insightful, and stimulating account after another, focusing on the relationship between our own and other species. Importantly, it reveals why traditional human-wildlife relations should be encouraged in a world that seeks to balance economic growth and environmental preservation."
— *John Noble Wilford in* The New York Times

ECO-BLUFF YOUR WAY TO GREENISM
THE GUIDE TO INSTANT ENVIRONMENTAL CREDIBILITY
Paul Spencer Sochaczewski
(writing as Paul Spencer Wachtel)
and Jeffrey A. McNeely
Bonus Books, Chicago, 1991
ISBN: 0-929387-22-8

The guide to attain quick and painless eco-credibility, with essential advice on things such as how to deal with people who prefer elephants to human beings, how to establish your street-cred by explaining the public relations coup of Chief Seattle, and how to stir up a party by roaring like an eco-guerilla.

"What a book! Covers insights into potentially disastrous global issues in a bright and enjoyable way. Takes no prisoners and opens our eyes to a new and more effective vision of the pathway to environmental sanity."
— *Noel Vietmeyer, US National Academy of Sciences*

The Sultan and the Mermaid Queen
Surprising Asian People, Places, and
Things that Go Bump in the Night
Editions Didier Millet, Singapore, 2008
ISBN: 978-981-4217-74-3

These 70 true, unnerving, off-the-radar Asian tales confirm Sochaczewski's unique voice as one of the leading travel writers of his generation. Why do Javanese sultans owe their power to the Mermaid Queen? Why are Indian villagers angry at the Monkey God Hanuman for not returning their sacred mountain? Why is the Indonesian island of Flores ground zero for "small people" fables? And why was the 90-year-old "last elephant hunter" of Vietnam offered a lucrative product endorsement?

"Sochaczewski is a world-class searcher, reporter, and observer … an insightful guide to an often obscure and rapidly changing world."
— *Christopher G. Moore, author of the Vincent Calvino novels*

"That rarest of writers — he has discovered an eternal assemblage of arcane explorers, putative emperors, frivolous mystics, sacrosanct elephants, and yes, miracle workers."
— *Harry Rolnick, author of* Spice Chronicles:
Exotic Tales of a Hungry Traveler

MALAYSIA
HEART OF SOUTHEAST ASIA
Archipelago Press, Singapore, 1991
ISBN 981-002733-8

This large-format book features spectacular specially commissioned images of 46 of the world's most famous photographers. Paul Spencer Sochaczewski (writing here as Paul Wachtel) wrote the accompanying text about the nature of Malaysia in the long section "Nature: The Goddess with a Thousand Faces."

(From the book)

A weak burst of heat lightning illuminates a two-meter leatherback turtle that has plodded ashore to lay her eggs, as her kind have done for millions of years ...

Nature in Malaysia is a Goddess of a Thousand Faces. People see in her what they wish — vulnerability, majesty, food, medicine, a cosmic balance, spirits, a business opportunity. People look at Nature and see themselves — warrior, hunter, hustler, worshipper, conqueror, voyager, parent, student, poet.

Nature has blessed Malaysia ...

About the Author

Bayang Penguang

Paul with Unding anak Libau, the almost-last shaman of Sarawak, a Malaysian state on the island of Borneo. Unding (90 years old when this photo was taken), a member of the Iban tribe, presents the author with a hand-drawn paper that he says will protect Paul's house from bad spirits. The guardian totem has been effective at safeguarding the author's house in Geneva, Switzerland, proving that white magic can traverse borders, cultures, and time zones.

Paul lives a quiet life in Geneva, Switzerland, riding his bike, growing tomatoes, making quince chutney, rereading science fiction classics of the 1950s that belonged to his father, and enjoying good wines without bothering to learn too much about them. Lacking the chance to scour Thailand's amulet markets, he has stopped collecting Ganeshas and has redirected his acquisition-gene toward garden centers. He is rewilding his backyard into an "enhanced woodland" filled with plants that are beneficial for all sorts of critters and nourishing for the universal human emotion of biophilia. He has some new quests planned but is reluctant to talk about them.